Seventy Times Seven

Zacchaeus Studies: New Testament

General Editor: Mary Ann Getty

Seventy Times Seven

Sin, Judgment, and Forgiveness in Matthew

by

Thomas W. Buckley

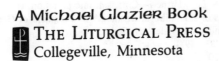

A Michael Glazier Book
THE LITURGICAL PRESS
Collegeville, Minnesota

ACKNOWLEDGEMENTS

The author is grateful to Michael Glazier for including this book in the *Zacchaeus Studies: New Testament Series.* Further thanks are due Herbert Kenny of Manchester, Massachusetts, and Patrick Flynn and Lenna Warner of Essex, Massachusetts, for their reading of the manuscript and helpful suggestions regarding style, and the staff of The Liturgical Press for their courtesies.

The Scripture quotations cited in this work are from the RSV (The New Oxford Annotated Bible, 1977).

1   2   3   4   5   6   7   8   9

Library of Congress Cataloging-in-Publication Data

Buckley, Thomas W., 1929-
    Seventy times seven : sin, judgment, and forgiveness in Matthew / Thomas W. Buckley.
        p.   cm. — (Zacchaeus studies. New Testament)
    "A Michael Glazier book."
    Includes bibliographical references.
    ISBN 0-8146-5686-2
    1. Bible. N.T. Matthew—Criticism, interpretation, etc.
    2. Forgiveness of sin—Biblical teaching. 3. Judgment of God-
-Biblical teaching. I. Title. II. Series.
BS2575.6.F6B83   1991
226.2'06—dc20
                                       90-25192
                                         CIP

In memory of
Thomas H. and Helen L. Buckley

Table of Contents

Editor's Note

Zacchaeus Studies provide concise, readable and relatively inexpensive scholarly studies on particular aspects of scripture and theology. The New Testament section of the series presents studies dealing with focal or debated questions; and the volumes focus on specific texts or particular themes of current interest in biblical interpretation. Specialists have their professional journals and other forums where they discuss matters of mutual concern, exchange ideas and further contemporary trends of research; and some of their work on contemporary biblical research is now made accessible for students and others in *Zacchaeus Studies.*

The authors in this series share their own scholarship in nontechnical language, in the areas of their expertise and interest. These writers stand with the best in current biblical scholarship in the English-speaking world. Since most of them are teachers, they are accustomed to presenting difficult material in comprehensible form without compromising a high level of critical judgment and analysis.

The works of this series are ecumenical in content and purpose and cross credal boundaries. They are designed to augment formal and informal biblical study and discussion. Hopefully they will also serve as texts to enhance and supplement seminary, university and college classes. The series will also aid Bible study groups, adult education and parish religious education classes to develop intelligent, versatile and challenging programs for those they serve.

Mary Ann Getty
New Testament Editor

Introduction

"Think not that I have come to abolish the law and the prophets; I have not come to abolish them but to fulfill them" (Mt 5:17). Thus the writer of the first canonical gospel recalls the mission of Jesus Christ. The words of the Lord signal the coming of the new age. The hope voiced by Israel's prophets for generations preceding would be at last fulfilled. For more than a thousand years ancient Israel had stood. By reason of its prophetic intuition of the living God and his will, the nation had embodied a tradition unparalleled in the long history of the human race. The fulfillment of that tradition the New Testament generally, and especially the first canonical gospel, sees in Jesus Christ. Israel of old would stand under judgment because it rejected the fulfillment of its own exalted tradition.

Almost a generation before the composition of Matthew's gospel the apostle Paul, writing of the events recorded in the Old Testament scriptures, says that "they were written down for our instruction, upon whom the end of the ages has come" (1 Cor 10:11). To the Romans he wrote that Christ is the "end of the law" (Rom 10:4), though in context, not only as successor to the law but as the true medium of that righteousness which the law could only pretend to impart. The eschatological perspective of Matthew, like that of the New Testament generally, is subservient to Christology. Again, the motif which acknowledges Jesus as the fulfillment of Israel's hope is especially strong in Matthew. His gospel includes at least forty-two explicit quotations from the Old Testament. We find only nineteen each in Mark and Luke and only fourteen in John. Of the Old Testament citations in Matthew, ten are introduced by a striking fulfillment formula which does not appear elsewhere in the synoptic gospels and only four times in John. Its key word is the passive of the Greek verb *plēroun,* "to fulfill." Thus Matthew introduces quotations at verses 1:22, 2:15, 17, 23, 4:14, 8:17, 12:17, 13:35, 21:4 and 27:9. Verse 2:5 is often added to this list, but because it is a saying of the scribes it naturally lacks the typical reference to fulfillment found in the other formula quotations.

Provenance

Matthew's gospel was probably written at Antioch in the eighth or ninth decade of the first century. Commonly regarded as the most Jewish of the gospels, it is finally set forth as a watershed both in Jewish and Christian history. To Christians, faith in Jesus as Lord had long been a touchstone for membership in the kingdom of heaven. Hence Jews and Jewish Christians had lived in uneasy tension. The Christians maintained themselves in Palestine and at the same time showed some deference to the Torah. The apostolic council appeared to recognize this when it commanded Christians to abstain not only from idolatry and unchastity but also "from what is strangled and from blood" (Acts 15:20). In the wake of the ill-fated revolt against Rome in the year 66 A.D. Judaism became more cautious and severe. The church would emerge even further from its Jewish matrix. In introducing the *Birkath Ha-Minim* or the twelfth benediction, so-called, into the synagogue service, the synod of Jamnia excommunicated Jewish Christians. The break was now complete though it had been long foreshadowed (cf. Gal 4:21-31). To a church whose roots were Jewish and whose founding generation was Jewish, would the charge raised at Jamnia ring true? Did Jesus abolish the law and the prophets? No, he fulfilled them. At the dawn of the Christian era, Philo could write of his own Jewish heritage, "We may fairly say that mankind from east to west, every country and nation and state, show aversion to foreign institutions. They think that they will enhance the respect for their own institutions by showing disrespect for those of other countries. It is not so with ours. They attract and win the attention of all, of barbarians, of Greeks, of nations of the east and the west, of Europe and Asia, of the whole inhabited world from end to end" (*Vita Mosis* II 12-20).[1] In spite of the anti-Semitism which sometimes appeared in the ancient world, a number of proselytes did adhere to Judaism.

Jesus of Nazareth, however, would authentically interpret the law and the prophets. With a view to the emergence of a renewed humanity he would actually heighten the demands of the law and the prophets. Through him would be fulfilled in the church the promise made to Abraham that his posterity would be as the sands of the seashore or the stars of the sky (Gen 22:17). It is Jesus who summons the generality of men and women to imitate the faith of Abraham and thus become the true children of their spiritual father. God could not be a god of the Jews alone. The universalism often voiced by the prophets (Is 2:2-4, 56:1-8, 60:1-14) is fulfilled finally through Jesus Christ whose farewell command is, "Go, therefore, and make disciples of all nations . . ." (Mt 28:18-20).

Author

To whom can be attributed the first canonical gospel with its deep sympathy for Jesus' forgiveness and love? Whoever was the final editor or redactor wrote after a long development of the text. An honored tradition of commentators' scrutiny or the work of "a scribal school" may have preceded the final redaction.[2] Most critics believe that the evangelist, like Luke, employed the gospel of Mark as well as an earlier collection of the sayings of Jesus called Q. He also made use of the tradition which had persevered within his own community. Some critics have suggested that an Aramaic source could have entered into the final composition of the gospel. To reconstruct that source, however, from the present Greek text is impossible.

---

[1]Philo, *Moses* (tr. F. H. Colson; Cambridge: Harvard University Press, 1966) II 19, 20. (Loeb Series).

[2]See K. Stendahl, *The School of St. Matthew* (2nd ed.; Lund: Gleerup, 1968).

Yet behind that source could have lain the authority of an apostle called Matthew, who in the gospel is identified with the tax collector whom Jesus calls in Matthew 10:3. In tradition the name of Matthew has persevered in association with the first canonical gospel. That it did so, suggests that Matthew was familiar to the church in Antioch and even as a revenue agent or tax collector (Mt 9:9, 10:3). In a gospel where the theme of forgiveness and reconciliation loomed large, the reminiscence of an apostle who as tax collector knew Jesus' forgiveness is certainly appropriate. As a tax collector, Matthew was a member of what in Palestine was a despised class. Among the Jews he could claim neither civil nor political rights. A quisling in the eyes of his people, he could not have thought himself other than a sinner before God. Another tax collector, Zacchaeus, protested perhaps overmuch: "Behold, Lord, the half of my goods I give to the poor; and if I have defrauded anyone of anything, I restore it fourfold" (Lk 19:8). The fourfold recompense can be understood in view of a prescription of the Jewish law, "four sheep for a 'stolen' sheep" (2 Sm 12:6). Zacchaeus was a Jew and knew the law. Thus did he seek vindication. But that could come only through Jesus Christ. And Matthew, Jesus calls to be his follower (Mt 9:9) and to join him at table (Mt 9:10). It was enormously magnanimous of Jesus.[3]

Antioch: An Early Christian Foundation

The mediation of divine forgiveness through Jesus should have influenced all whom it touched, that they in turn might be ready to forgive. The vigor of the church in Antioch had been long assured, yet, as in early Christian foundations elsewhere, unity was more something to be aspired to than actually achieved.[4] Antioch was the scene of the confrontation between Peter and Paul over the matter of table fellowship among Jewish and Gentile Christians (Gal 2:11-14). Peter had eaten with the Gentiles but upon the arrival of emissaries from Jerusalem and James, he demurred,

---

[3] J. Jeremias, *Jerusalem in the Time of Jesus* (tr. F. H. & C. H. Cave; London: SCM Press, 1969) 124, 126.

[4] See Rom 14-15:1-13, 1 Cor 12-14, Gal 5:2-15.

an action probably rooted in his pastoral sense. He wanted to avoid trouble with "the circumcision party." In fact his action would have pleased the Judaizers, who at that time threatened Christian liberty. But the threat passed. By the time Matthew writes, the voice of the Judaizers would have been much muted. Jerusalem had fallen. In the wake of the ill-fated Jewish revolt in 66 A.D. a sense of the "mother church" had been transferred from Jerusalem to Rome. Jesus' sentiment, which the evangelist probably derived from the Q source, that "not what goes into the mouth defiles a man" (Mt 15:11) appears to echo an earlier polemic against the Mosaic code. In fulfilling the law and the prophets Jesus reinterpreted them and actually heightened their demand, but in the name of love not in the name of an exaggerated legalism.

Furthermore, for the Judaizing element in the primitive church, the Gentile mission would be perilous to the Old Testament heritage unless at the same time the Mosaic code were set forth. The Messiah's first claim was upon the house of Israel. Yet as Matthew delineates the public ministry of Jesus Christ, his mission is extended through the twelve to the church. While the mission of the apostles is identified with the historical mission of Jesus Christ to the lost sheep of the house of Israel (Mt 10:6, 15:24), it will be extended beyond, and not only in particular circumstances as with Jesus (Mt 15:21-28) but generally and universally (Mt 28:18, 19). The twelve will bear witness before governors and kings (Mt 10:11). To men and women, however, whose manner of adherence to the church was conditioned by their own past, be it Jewish or pagan, Matthew emphasized forbearance and forgiveness.

Though Matthew alone of the synoptic writers speaks of the church as *ekklēsia* or congregation, church order and structure is not a preoccupation. But he does insist upon a spirit of forbearance and forgiveness without which the advantage of any church order would be compromised and Christians themselves subject to stringent judgment. Some years would pass before Ignatius would oversee the church in Antioch as bishop. The earlier church order to which Luke alludes in the Acts of the Apostles 13:1-3 admitted the leadership of prophets and teachers.

In some cases these charismatic figures apparently became false prophets and sources of trouble. Matthew does not mention factions, as Paul did earlier in his first letter to the Corinthians (1 Cor 11:19), but he does indict the false prophets unreservedly (Mt 7:15-23). They were threatening the faith of the community. They will somehow carry on even to the last days when by "leading many astray" they will increase the anguish of the elect (Mt 24:10-12). Many were being led astray in the first days of the church. Hence in the opinion of many commentators the evangelist was addressing a divided community.⁵ He urges forbearance and forgiveness, even as he warns of judgment.

According to Matthew, Jesus bids his followers pray, ". . . Forgive us our debts, as we also have forgiven our debtors" (Mt 6:12). Mark (11:25) and Luke (11:4) read similarly. The compassion and forgiveness of our heavenly Father is to be reflected in the disposition of his children towards one another. This is borne out by the reiteration of this one petition at the conclusion of the Lord's prayer (Mt 6:14, 15) and still further, by the parable of the unmerciful servant (Mt 18:23-35) which is unique to Matthew. Both the reiteration of the petition and the parable admonish men to relieve their debtors. At the conclusion of the Lord's prayer (Mt 6:14, 15) "debt" becomes "trespass" and by implication, debtor becomes trespasser. "Trespass" would seem a more likely term for an offense against God but in latter day Judaism, for example in the Septuagint and the Targums, "debt" becomes a common term for sin. So deep was Jewry's sense of indebtedness to God.

Forgiveness and Church Order

In the discourse on the church and church order forgiveness occupies a surprising prominence (Mt 18:1-19:1). The eighteenth chapter of Matthew divides itself into a twofold consideration, each one closing with reference to the Father in heaven (Mt 18:14,

---

⁵Cf. W. Thompson, *Matthew's Advice to a Divided Community* (Rome: Biblical Institute Press, 1970). _____ with E. LaVerdiere, "New Testament Communities in Transition: A Study of Matthew and Luke," *TS* 37 (1976) 567-597.

35).[6] The sense of God as our father looms large in Matthew, more so than in Mark and Luke. In this gospel Jesus invites his followers to share with him the fatherhood of God. His father is their father, the father of the poor in spirit, of the meek and the sorrowful, of the persecuted and dispossessed, of all to whom he would reveal himself through Jesus and who would inherit the kingdom of heaven (Mt 5:3-12, 11:5). Jesus' very language is preserved in the earliest documents of the New Testament. Through the Spirit, Christians can call God Abba or Father (Gal 4:6, Rom 8:15). The living God who once revealed himself to Moses as essential being (Ex 3:14), the God of Abraham, Isaac, and Jacob, is now revealed as our Father and so acknowledged by the primitive Christian community. The blessing which Paul conveyed to Christian churches and to Philemon was early on a familiar one: "Grace to you, and peace from God our Father and the Lord Jesus Christ." Such grace and peace would be the privilege of children of the heavenly Father and of the brethren of the Lord Jesus Christ. Our Father in heaven is the ground of the church's existence, and guarantor of that order which would provide for his "little ones" and among them and their leaders foster forbearance and forgiveness. It is not his will that "anyone of these little ones should perish" (Mt 18:14). It is his will that they and their leaders forgive their brethren from the heart (Mt 18:35).

The question put by Peter to Jesus, "Lord, how often shall my brother sin against me, and I forgive him? As many as seven times?" (Mt 18:21, 22) suggests Peter's generosity but even more the influence of Jesus' word and example. A light was dawning to penetrate the hearts of men darkened as they had been since man first swore vengeance seventy-times-seven-fold on his fellow man (Gen 4:24). In answering Peter's question Jesus alludes to that dark hour when the sword was introduced into history and man's lust for retaliation and vengeance was quickened beyond

---

[6]W. Pesch, "Die sogenannte Gemeinde ordnung Mt 18," *BZ* 7 (1963) 22–235 Cf. also W. Trilling, *Das wahre Israel: Studien zur Theologie des Matthäus Evangeliums* (München: Kosel-Verlag, 1964) 106–123.

all bounds.[7] But a new covenant between God and man had been introduced in Jesus' blood (Mt 26:28) and in its light and love forgiveness could be offered without stint. "I do not say to you seven times, but seventy times seven," said Jesus (Mt 18:22). The love issuing from the new covenant would be cast in ever more dramatic relief as sin persevered and with it the peril of judgment.

The New Covenant and the Forgiveness of Sins

To Matthew the forgiveness of sins is inherent in the inauguration of the new covenant. The actual reference to "forgiveness of sins" appears more frequently in Luke, both in his gospel and in the Acts of the Apostles. Luke uses the phrase initially in connection with John the Baptist (Lk 1:77, 3:3).[8] In truth the main mission of the Baptist was to preach to his contemporaries salvation coming through Jesus Christ. He was the precursor. He evoked past deliverance of the nation Israel from captivity but at the same time he signalled the coming deliverance of all humanity from the more grievous bondage of sin and death. Only once does Matthew use the phrase "unto the forgiveness of sins" and that in the most solemn moment of the last supper when Jesus commences the expiatory sacrifice whose consummation he would achieve on the Cross (Mt 26:28).

From the beginning the motif of forgiveness is woven into the fabric of the first canonical gospel like a golden thread. It is not the central theme of the gospel nor even a dominant theme but such as are the dominant themes would each encompass forgiveness. The high Christology of the gospel, that Jesus is the Son of God even as he is the Son of David; the fulfillment of the law and the prophets; the introduction of the kingdom and foundation of the church; these are overriding themes. In the development of each, the quality of mercy and forgiveness would have an appropriate place. The characterization of Jesus as Son of David may not convey in itself the thought of forgiveness, yet

[7]See G. Von Rad, *Old Testament Theology* (tr. D. M. G. Stalker; 2 vols.; London: Oliver & Boyd, 1962) I 155.

[8]Lk 1:77, 3:3, 24:47; Acts 2:38, 5:31, 10:43, 13:38, 26:18.

it is the compassionate stance of the legendary king which Matthew recalls.⁹ As the Son of God, Jesus is the embodiment of divine mercy. Hence he forgives sins. In founding the church, he grants it the power to bind or to loose; it is to be a new community whose members are charged to forgive one another. The call to repentance attends the introduction of the kingdom (Mt 3:2, 4:17), and it is an eschatologically grounded call which, when acknowledged, admits the grace of forgiveness.¹⁰

Man was thoroughly immersed in sin. In divine forgiveness alone lay hope. Sin is stated as a power less dramatically in the synoptic gospels than in John, and less so than in Paul, where sin like death is personified and invested with an apocalyptic aura. "So the law is holy, and the commandment is holy and just and good" (Rom 7:12), yet it can lead to death, wrote Paul. So powerful is sin that it could pervert the very oracle of God. So powerful is sin, that once quickened at the instance of law, it can lead one to assume a lawless or a law-abiding posture. But pride can be indulged in either case and thus lead to death. How so? To Paul, the answer lies in man himself. If death can define the situation of man, then so too does sin. "We know that the law is spiritual; but I am carnal, sold under sin" (Rom 7:14). Thus starkly does Paul describe our human bondage. The thoroughness of that bondage he probes in the balance of chapter seven in Romans. Only God's forgiveness and grace can resolve the dialectic between even divine law and sin in terms other than despair. Jesus would mediate divine forgiveness and grace. Though sin is not as dramatically stated as a power in the synoptics as in Paul, retribution due sin is set forth. Of the one hundred and forty-eight literary units or pericopes which can be counted in Matthew, sixty refer to judgment. Yet, according to Matthew, Jesus taught that in his mercy God would temper his judgment. The blood of Jesus would be poured out for many, viz., for the *hoi polloi* or the generality of men and women.

---

⁹D. Duling, "The Therapeutic Son of David: An Element in Matthew's Christological Apologetic," *NTS* 24 (1978) 392-410.

¹⁰G. Strecker, *Der Weg der Gerechtigheit* (Göttingen: Vandenhoeck & Ruprecht, 1971) 148-149.

Who constitutes the generality of men and women but such as tax collectors and sinners and the crowd who do not know the law and therefore stood accursed in the eyes of the righteous? (Jn 7:49). Yet it is they, the tax collectors and sinners and in Hebrew, *'am ha'aretz* or the people of the land whom Jesus addresses. That Jesus would eat with such provoked the Pharisees (Mt 9:11). The charge would then be made that he was even their friend (Mt 11:19). And when the conflict between Jesus and the religious authorities of Judaism became irreversible, Jesus told them that "tax collectors and harlots" would enter the kingdom of God before the spiritual leaders of Israel (Mt 21:31). "For John came to you in the way of righteousness, and you did not believe him but the tax collectors and the harlots believed him . . ." (Mt 21:32). They believed and repented. Humility before grace! Rather than that self-righteousness which is no righteousness at all, it is the contrite and humble heart which invites the compassion and righteousness of God.

Jesus receives tax collectors and sinners in the name of mercy. Unique to Matthew is the recollection of the prophet Hosea to underscore how Jesus' mercy is consistent with the will of God. The sentiment pervades section 9:10 through 9:34 which appropriately follows the healing of the paralytic and the forgiveness of sins. Employing a rabbinic formula, Jesus advises his adversaries, "Go and learn what this means, 'I desire mercy and not sacrifice' " (Mt 9:13, Hos 6:6).

The sacrifice implied in deference to the prescriptions of the Torah must on occasion yield to the imperative of mercy. Notwithstanding Matthew's respect for the law, its prescription in reference to table fellowship (Mt 9:10, 11), and fasting (Mt 9:14, 15), and the ritually unclean (Mt 9:18-26), could be abrogated in the name of that divine compassion which Jesus would mediate to all. Divine compassion lay behind the king's free and universal invitation to the great banquet (Mt 22:1-14). The object of Jesus' healings include suppliants beyond the community of the Torah or the law, for example, tax collectors, as well as the ritually unclean or disabled. All that is asked of them is faith, humility, and contriteness of heart. These, Jesus will gather into a new community: the church.

1

Sin and the First Canonical Gospel

What is this sin which, apart from Jesus, can define the existential situation of man? For it is Jesus alone who saves his people from their sins (Mt 1:21). His blood is poured out for the forgiveness of sins (Mt 26:28). Though the synoptic writers do not address the origin of sin as profoundly as Paul nor cast it so dramatically as a power unleashed at the dawn of human history (Rom 5:12), they concede that sin is pervasive and powerful. Its presence is consistently acknowledged. Luke joins Matthew in indicting a "faithless and perverse generation" (Lk 9:41). To Matthew the generation was evil and adulterous (Mt 12:39, 16:4). This description of the generation as adulterous represents a Matthean redaction. They were "adulterous" in the Old Testament sense where idolatry is described as adultery before God. Indeed it is the idolatry of man with its implicit ungodliness which both the book of Wisdom and Paul see as carrying in its wake further sinfulness by way of retribution (Wis 1:16, Rom 1:18-32).

Hamartia

To probe further the mystery of sin, its origin and nature, was not to the purpose of the synoptic writers. Its existential reality was evident enough in the multiplicity of sins which men can commit against God and against their fellow man. In the synoptic gospels the word which is used most frequently for sin is *hamartia*. It derives from a verb meaning to fall short, or to miss the mark. Its moral or religious meaning had developed in the Septuagint or Greek Old Testament when the word was employed to translate the Hebrew *ḥaṭa'* or offense against God. In the synoptic gospels and in the Acts of the Apostles *hamartia* is understood as an individual act issuing from one's own heart, but since the sins of men are many and varied it is always found in the plural. Fundamentally *hamartia* represents a heart recalcitrant to admit grace. Apart from grace the human heart must still beat in the darkness and shame of a fallen race. Thus hatred and impure desire become tantamount in seriousness to murder and adultery (Mt 5:21-28). Jesus makes his own the word of Isaiah on the opposition of lips and heart (Mt 15:7-9, cf. Isa 29:13). He teaches that man is defiled not by what enters the mouth but by that which comes out and proceeds from the heart. "For out of the heart comes evil thoughts, murder, adultery, fornication, theft, false witness, slander" (Mt 15:19). These derive from what is in Hebrew the *yetzer ha-ra* or evil impulse[1] which in rabbinical tradition is enthroned in the heart. Yet from the consequence of that impulse and from the impulse itself Jesus comes to save us. That he should first offer forgiveness for what derives from the heart leads directly to the transformation of one's heart, and enables man to forgive his brother "from his heart" (Mt 18:35). It leads to purity of heart, the blessing reserved for inheritors of the kingdom of heaven (Mt 5:8).

Indebtedness to God

The religious sense of sin was also expressed in Judaism by the word *opheilēma,* meaning debt. This figurative meaning would have been alien to the Graeco-Roman world but in Judaism, in the Septuagint and the Targums, "debt" became a common term for sin. Such was the Jewish sense of indebtedness to God. The petition in the Lord's prayer ". . . Forgive us our debts, as we also have forgiven our debtors," (Mt 6:12) is repeated in Matthew at the conclusion of the prayer (Mt 6:14, 15). In the latter case, however, the usage becomes *paraptōma,* meaning here a transgression or trespass against God or against men. As our Father in heaven forgives us our trespasses, Jesus bids his disciples for-

[1] Gen 6:5, 8:21.

bear their peers not only their frailty and need but even that reprehensible conduct which could fall under moral condemnation.[2] In the initial petition the disciple prays ". . . Forgive our debts" (Mt 6:12). The Old Testament conveyed a deep sense of man's indebtedness to God. There is nothing which man has which God has not given him. Even so, the gifts of life and liberty are often unacknowledged or subverted from their purpose. For faith, man returns doubt and disobedience; for hope, despair, and for love, hatred. We cannot pay our debts. Hence our petition that God forgive them. He does forgive them at that supreme hour in all history when Jesus dies on the Cross. In the Matthean redaction Jesus' blood is shed "for the forgiveness of sins" (Mt 26:28). On that day when the earth trembled and the dead rose (Mt 27:51-54) in token of the new age and the inauguration of the kingdom a further blessing appropriate to the new age was introduced among men and women: the forgiveness of sins. With it comes the call to forgive our fellow man especially that debt of love which without grace, man cannot render (Mt 5:23-26, 43-48, cf. 18:23-35). Through such a disposition to forgive will this world be touched with heavenly grace and the kingdom augmented.

Anomia

In Jewish tradition, in Genesis and in the apocryphal literature, Satan is the tempter in the garden of Eden. He speaks through the serpent. He tempts our progenitors to become "like God, knowing good and evil" (Gen 3:5). He thus tempts Adam and Eve to subvert the order between creator and creature, to achieve for themselves moral autonomy. The book of Wisdom reiterates the argument (Wis 2:24, cf. 1:16). So too does Paul (2 Cor 11:3)— though in his classic address to that disobedience "which brought death into the world and all our woe," he does not recall the link between the devil and original sin (Rom 5:12). In Genesis the serpent was introduced to question Eve, thus to emphasize the

---

[2]A. von Schlatter, *Der Evangelist Matthäus* (3 Aufl.; Stuttgart: Calwer Verlag, 1948) 217.

demonic nature of utter skepticism which would overreach even the limit inherent in creatureliness in its pursuit of knowledge. To Paul it is man himself who is responsible. His origin may have been from the dust but he is created to be free and to be thus distinguished from the rest of brute creation. Paul, however, would not deny the reality of the demonic nor depreciate its influence. Sin is delineated precisely in Satan's "Non serviam!" The "why" of this stance before God is beyond reason, and remains within a realm of mystery surpassed only by the greater mystery of God's grace. The revelation of the greater mystery awaited Jesus Christ, yet it remains a mystery: the dispensation of grace, the call and justification of sinners. In its radical sense sin as *anomia* affronts the law. *Anomia,* that is, *nomos* or law with the alpha privative, means either the denial or transgression of law. In the biblical context the connection with law is somewhat attenuated,[3] since *anomia* attains a broader scope and means sin or evil. In the Septuagint it became practically synonymous with *hamartia.* It contradicts the will of our Father in heaven. According to Matthew the scribes and the Pharisees were filled with hypocrisy and iniquity or *anomia* (Mt 23:28). It is not as though they were living apart from or without the law, but in their tithing of mint and dill and cummin they neglected "the weightier matters of the law, justice and mercy and faith" (Mt 23:23). They thus neglected the will of our Father in heaven. They were hypocrites. Behind their masks of religious pretension, pride and self-righteousness vitiated the true beginning of religious sentiment, namely, the humility and contriteness of heart without which men and women cannot begin their approach to God. Iniquitous, they neglected the weightier matters of the law. Just as the golden rule (Mt 7:12), and the two great commandments (Mt 22:38-40), summarily express the law and the prophets, so too do "justice and mercy and faith." For all their meticulous observance of the Torah and its 613 distinct statutes and decrees, the Pharisees could not see the forest because of the trees. They neglected "justice and mercy and faith." Similarly they are indicted in Luke, though there for neglecting justice and the love of God (Lk 11:42).

---

[3] W. D. Davies, *The Sermon on the Mount* (Cambridge University Press, 1964) 205-208.

Matthew notes the neglect of mercy. He does so consistently but by way of contrast to Jesus' compassion and forgiveness. When the scribes and the Pharisees are denounced as hypocrites and iniquitous, the language recalls the earlier reprobation of false prophets, exorcists, and wonder workers at the conclusion of Jesus' Sermon on the Mount (Mt 7:15-23). Both the Pharisees and false prophets within the nascent church were guilty of *anomia,* or of a fundamentally rebellious disposition towards God. Self-assured even before God, assertive in their own works, they did not do the will of our Father in heaven. Therein is defined the shape and contour of sin.

The law is holy and the commandment is holy, just, and good (Rom 7:12). Yet so powerful is sin, so powerful is that latent hostility to God which informed man at the Fall (Rom 8:7, 8), that sin can pervert the oracle of God. What was meant to lead to life, leads rather to death. Thus does Paul present sin; and similarly is the Johannine concept of sin as a power presented in the fourth gospel. The synoptic gospels do not purport, however, to probe the origin and nature of sin. It was enough to set forth its existential reality. That sin was a pervasive reality argued to its power. Hence a sense of its power must be implicit when sin is described as *anomia.* Again, *anomia* cannot be understood simply in relation to a question of law. It has a much broader meaning. It contradicts God's will and counsel, and God's will, with its creative dynamism working itself out in nature, cannot be rejected with impunity. Who has resisted God and found peace?

Matthew refers to *anomia* as sin for the last time in Jesus' discourse on the end of Jerusalem and on the end of the world. "Because wickedness is multiplied, most men's love will grow cold" (Mt 24:12). The reference is an addition to the Markan tradition. Similarly stands the reference to the false prophets in this immediate context (Mt 24:11). In a series of brief but ominous warnings at the conclusion of the Sermon on the Mount the evangelist had recalled the warnings by Jesus about false prophets (Mt 7:15). They were among those in the early church who though graced to prophesy, to exorcise the demonic, and to work miracles, would in the end be judged workers of evil. This, because they neither sought out, nor fulfilled the will of our Father in heaven (Mt.

7:21-23). Here in Jesus' eschatological discourse their appearance is coincidental with the increasing prevalence of evil. Christians had already been warned that in the last days the mystery of evil or the *mystērion tēs anomias* would burgeon forth. It was already at work (2 Thess 2:7). That it should finally be revealed was consistent with apocalyptic speculation on the last days. For the sake of the elect the last days will be shortened (Mt 24:22). *Anomia* or sin will be rampant in proportion to the increasing malice of men before the deluge (Gen 6:5) or to the depravity of Sodom and Gomorrah (Gen 18:20). In its pervasiveness sin and evil will contaminate even the church. Christians are warned of harassment and persecution from without; of confusion and betrayal from within (Mt 24:9-14). "Most men's love will grow cold" (Mt 24:12). Except for one instance in Luke this usage for love appears only here in the synoptic gospels: *agapē,* a truly selfless love of God and neighbor. It will grow cold in the last days when the world itself will be gripped in the chill of its impending demise. *Agapē* is a grace, comparable to a fire "which many waters cannot quench, nor floods drown" (Cant 8:7). In the last days the splendor of such love will fade and its power weaken. Beneath the noxious influence of evil, ties of affection will dissolve. Such dissolution would again be characteristic of the apocalyptic genre which dominates Jesus' discourse on the end of the age. To the evangelist, dissension in his own church could have made the tragic vision of apocalyptic the more credible.[4]

Workers of Evil

Before the "workers of evil" (Mt 7:23, 13:41) looms the day of judgment, a dark and fatal prospect. If the punishment ordained is proportionate to the crime, then how fearful must be the essence of sin. Jesus' Sermon on the Mount culminates in his enunciating the Golden Rule, "So whatever you wish that men would do to you, do so to them; for this is the law and the prophets" (Mt 7:12). Then there follows a series of brief but ominous warnings. The evangelist makes clear that the followers

---

[4]John P. Meier, *The Vision of Matthew* (New York: Paulist Press, 1979) 169.

of Jesus are to enter by the narrow gate and follow the way which leads to life, howsoever arduous. The way that leads to destruction and its gate, is wide (Mt 7:13, 14). Upon that way tread hypocrites and fools whom the evangelist goes on to contrast with the true and the wise (Mt 7:15-27). The language of Jesus becomes apocalyptic. Both fire and flood is promised those who will not hear and obey his words (Mt 7:24), who contradict the will of the Father in heaven (Mt 7:21). Fire and flood bespeak the last judgment and the chaos to which this age and its adherents must be delivered upon hearing the awful sentence ". . . I never knew you: depart from me, you workers of evil" (Mt 7:23). The entire context (Mt 7:13-27) is permeated with the sense that with the coming of the kingdom and the new age, the judgment also is at hand. The judgment will encompass all. Even the disciples of Jesus stand in peril of spiritual presumption. Like the Pharisees who boasted of their adherence to Abraham their father but rejected the repentance necessary to enter into the kingdom, so too those who boast of their adherence to Christ and cry our "Lord, Lord!", but fail to bring forth the "fruits of repentance" and to do the will of the heavenly Father, they too will meet the sentence reserved for workers of evil (Mt 3:7-10, 7:5-23). Matthew's strongest invective is directed against the spiritual authorities of contemporary Judaism, the scribes and the Pharisees (chapter 23). How ominous is the warning directed to the leaders within the church who, though graced with the spiritual powers of prophecy, exorcism, and healing, can still be judged finally workers of evil. This is because they neither sought out nor fulfilled the will of the heavenly Father (Mt 7:21-23).

The scribes and the Pharisees would fill up the measure of their fathers (Mt 23:32). Sons of those who murdered the prophets they would themselves shed the blood of the latter day emissaries of God whom Jesus sends forth, "prophets and wise men and scribes" (Mt 23:34). The last of the seven woes is pronounced and the terrible curse is uttered, "Upon you may come all the righteous blood shed on earth, from the blood of innocent Abel to the blood of Zechariah the son of Barachiah, whom you murdered between the sanctuary and the altar" (Mt 23:35, cf. Gen 4:8, 2 Chr 24:20-22). The centuries coalesce, blood commingles;

and the antagonists of Jesus fill up the measure of their fathers. The proprietors of the nation shed the blood of the righteous, even the very embodiment of righteousness, Jesus Christ. They scourge or slay "the prophets and wise men and scribes" whom he sends forth and thus they resist incarnate Wisdom (1 Cor 2:6-8) even as they sinned against the Holy Spirit (Mt 12:31, 32).

The Unforgiveable Sin

Few texts in the New Testament are as challenging both as to form and substance as those relating to blasphemy against the Spirit, and the unforgiveable sin (Mt 12:31, 32, cf. Lk 12:10, Mk 3:28, 29). "Therefore I tell you, every sin and blasphemy will be forgiven men, but the blasphemy against the Spirit will not be forgiven. And whoever says a word against the Son of Man will be forgiven; but whoever speaks against the Holy Spirit will not be forgiven either in this age or in the age to come." The evangelist Mark does not speak of the Son of Man but simply of the sons of men. ". . . All sins will be forgiven the sons of men, and whatever blasphemies they utter" (Mk 3:28). Matthew and Luke speak of the Son of Man also and though a word against him may be forgiven, blasphemy against the Spirit implies a conscious stance so profoundly averse to grace and forgiveness it is simply unforgiveable. In this one instance the announcement of universal forgiveness is qualified. Blasphemy against the Holy Spirit is unforgiveable. The concept of an unforgiveable sin actually appears elsewhere in the New Testament, both in Hebrews and the first letter of John (Heb 6:4-6, 1 John 5:16). In Matthew it jars, this evangelist so much emphasizes Jesus' forgiveness. As a result, some have suggested that the verse referring to the sin against the Holy Spirit was something introduced by the community, or that the whole pericope with its balance (Mt 12:31, 32) reflected a prophetic oracle. Even if this were so, however, the early Christian prophets would hardly have created their oracles *ex nihilo*. They would have expanded material deriving ultimately from Jesus.[5]

[5]C. Colpe, "Der Spruch von der Lästerung des Geistes," *Der Ruf Jesu und die Antwort der Gemeinde* (ed. E. Lohse; Göttingen: Vandenhoeck & Ruprecht, 1971) 45; M. E. Boring

The sentence, that for blasphemy against the Spirit there is no forgiveness either in this world or in the world to come, is set against an ominous background. In the context of the gospel the warning is raised as the conspiracy of the spiritual leaders of Judaism against Jesus deepened. It would surface finally in the calumnious charge that it was Jesus who conspired and that with the devil (Mt 12:24). The deep malice of the charge can be gauged by this, that in the law a sorcerer was liable to death. That the charge was tantamount to blasphemy against the Spirit with its prospect of unrelenting retribution (cf. Mt 23:33) is perhaps the severest warning in the New Testament but not without precedent in the Old. The provocation was ancient, though now more critical, not only because it was directed against Jesus but against Jesus as revealing the dynamic of the kingdom, that is, the Spirit of God (Mt 12:28). Through the Spirit, Jesus exorcises demonic power and forgives sin. To deny this is blasphemy against the Spirit and provocative of the sentence of condemnation.

To the Jewish world contemporary with Jesus and then with the evangelist, blasphemy against the Spirit was not something wholly new. In Jewish tradition Moses was prophet *par excellence*. As a prophet he would have labored under the Spirit. To rabbinical tradition the Holy Spirit was in the first instance the prophetic spirit. Yet Moses was rebuked as the generation of the wilderness murmured against the Lord at Massah and Meribah and then apostatized before the Holy Mountain. Such was the tragic pattern of resistance to the Spirit which would fester in Israel, now latently, now openly, until finally it erupts against Jesus, the anointed of the Spirit. Such resistance had brought down the nation before and would do so again, not only the nation but "whosoever speaks against the Holy Spirit." The increasing malice of the conspiracy against Jesus issued in calumny. Hence he uttered his warning (Mt 12:32).

Implicit in that warning is the call to decision. It sounds beyond Jesus' own times, beyond the struggle of the Matthean com-

"The Unforgiveable Sin Logion Mark III 28–29/Matt XII 31–32/Luke XII 10: Formal Analysis and History of the Tradition," *NT* 18 (1976) 277. The latter would ascribe the second half of v 32 to the church.

munity with the synagogue. It will reecho as long as men would prefer any other explanation of the inexplicable, be it natural, preternatural, even demonic, rather than to admit the possibility of divine intervention in human affairs.[6] Implicit in this warning is the call to decide for Jesus as mediator of the Holy Spirit. It surely follows from the verse immediately preceding with its clear either-or, "He who is not with me is against me and he who does not gather with me scatters" (Mt 12:30).

The generation that rejected Jesus Christ as its Messiah, and then rejected his "prophets, wise men, and scribes" (Mt 23:34), would prove to be the last of ancient Israel. In September of the year 70 Jerusalem fell to the tenth legion under Titus Vespasian. The city was leveled and the temple brought down. Israel of old, which had as its religious and civil center the city of David, ceased to exist. Yet it was from the Jews that had come the leaders of the early church. Indeed, Matthew writes his gospel, partly to reassure a church whose roots were Jewish and whose founding generation was Jewish that the charge raised by the rabbinate convoked at Jamnia was not true; Jesus did not come to abolish the law and the prophets. He came rather to fulfil them.

The Parable of the Weeds in the Wheat

So strong is its substance, so pervasive its growth, sin cannot be extirpated until the end of the world and the final passage of the present age. The workers of evil are compared to so many weeds which in their aggressive growth and entanglement touch the sons of the kingdom (Mt 13:38). In the parable of the wheat and the weeds the householder is asked by his servants, "Do you want us to go and gather them?" "No", he said, "lest in gathering the weeds you uproot the wheat along with them" (Mt 13:29). Both the parable (Mt 13:24-30) and its interpretation are unique to Matthew (Mt 13:36-43). Its inspiration may have been a growing sense that a mélange of good and evil will characterize the existence of the church. The interpretation reflects the time after

---

[6]E. Schweizer, *The Good News according to Matthew* (tr. David E. Green; Atlanta: John Knox, 1975) 289.

Christ when the field of missionary endeavor had become increasingly the world (Mt 13:38). The church found more and more within its sphere the generality of men and women.

The parable itself, though somewhat elaborated in the course of its transmission, found its inspiration in Jesus. Its original thrust remains: the coming judgment and that alone will finally separate the weeds from the wheat. Judgment is reserved to the last. For all that the imagery of the parable suggests about sin and evil, its strength, its aggressive and entangling growth, does not the parable say something about the forbearance of Jesus and his readiness to forgive? Had Jesus been a Pharisee he would likely have called for the prompt extirpation of the weeds: similarly, had he been an apocalyptic visionary or even a zealot. Jesus, however, who came not to call the righteous but sinners (Mt 9:13), would bear with the weeds. He told his disciples, "Love your enemies and pray for those who persecute you . . ." (Mt 5:44). He rebuked James and John when they would bring fire upon the unfriendly Samaritans (Lk 9:51-55). He would show forbearance to sinners.

This is not to diminish the seriousness with which Jesus envisioned the coming judgment. In the interpretation of the parable of the wheat and the weeds, the closing of the present age dominates the evangelist's consideration. Then the weeds, the evil doers, will be separated from the good seed, the sons and daughters of the kingdom. As the purging transpires within the flames of the last day the righteous will survive transfigured in the kingdom of the Father (Mt 13:43). The forbearance which the parable itself enjoined upon the servants of the householder is no longer at issue. In the light of the interpretation, such exhortation to the community as does exist must derive from consideration of the coming judgment. This should strengthen our sense of the divine call in the present. "He who has ears, let him hear" (Mt 13:43).

2

Peril of Judgment

From the beginning of the public ministry of Jesus, his words and works were full of promise and yet at the same time were fraught with peril to men and nations, even Israel. His preaching and miracles summoned men and women to decide for or against him, for salvation or judgment. One day all will answer for sin. Of the one hundred and forty-eight pericopes or literary units which can be counted in Matthew at least sixty refer to judgment.[1] Much more than in Mark or Luke, Matthew's vocabulary shows words or expressions which belong to the threat or warning of judgment. Only Matthew contains detailed descriptions of the last judgment: 25:31ff., 13:36ff., and 7:21ff. Thus the motif of judgment is a salient one in the first canonical gospel. It relates to the gospel's dominant themes. The high Christology of the gospel which emphasizes Jesus' divinity is enhanced through the portrayal of Jesus as the universal and final judge. Fulfillment of the law and the prophets reposes in Jesus and the church as ancient Israel is judged. In time, at the last assize, the church itself will answer for its government and members.

"Repent, for the Kingdom of Heaven is at Hand"

The passing tradition of the law and the prophets found renewed voice, first in the word of the Baptist, then in that of Jesus who in fulfilling the old, sets forth the new. "Repent, for

---

[1]D. Marguerat, *Le Jugement dans l'Évangile de Matthieu* (Geneva: Labor et Fides, 1981) 52.

the kingdom of heaven is at hand" (Mt 3:7, 4:17). What Jesus taught in the name of the kingdom caused astonishment among the people (Mt 7:28). What he wrought in the name of the kingdom even his enemies conceded derived from a power greater than man's. Hence the peril involved in rejecting him is voiced again and again. A series of brief and ominous warnings conclude the Sermon on the Mount (Mt 7:13-27). Fire and flood are promised those who will not hear and obey the words of Jesus.

Accusatory Voices from the Past

In reconstructing the Sermon on the Mount, Matthew suggests that Jesus spoke *to the crowds* (Mt 5:1, 7:28). The evangelist thus hinted at the universal pertinence of Jesus' reinterpretation of the law and the prophets. Speaking more directly to the Jews and in response to their request for some sign of vindication, Jesus warned them that at the judgment the people of Nineveh and then the queen of the South would arise to condemn Jesus' own generation. Matthew is following Q at this point, though the evangelist does interpose a verse (Mt 12:40) in the light of Jesus' resurrection from the dead. To the evangelist Jonah's "three days and three nights in the belly of the whale" (Mt 12:40, Jonah 2:1) prefigured Jesus' own burial. That Jonah was delivered prefigured the resurrection of Jesus from the dead. The resurrection authenticated Jesus' preaching and enhanced dramatically the sign of Jonah. As Jonah was delivered from the whale and the watery depths, so was Jesus from the realm of the dead. In the Q source which both Matthew and Luke adopt, the "sign" is simply the prophet Jonah and his preaching. At Jonah's preaching the word of God penetrated the walls of fabled Nineveh. Its people repented. But the generation to which Jesus preached, did not repent even though in Jesus there was someone greater than Jonah (Mt 12:41). The intervention of Jonah and the prophets was tentative compared to that of Jesus whose visitation was eschatological, that is, signalling the beginning of the end of the present age, and therefore decisive for salvation or judgment. At the judgment, the Ninevites will rise with Jesus' generation and condemn it. They will arise and condemn all who would answer Jesus with incredulity and impenitence.

Similarly will the queen of the South indict Jesus' adversaries. "For she came from the ends of the earth to hear the wisdom of Solomon and behold, something greater than Solomon is here" (Mt 12:42). Jesus who was a prophet and yet more than a prophet (Mt 12:41) surpassed in his wisdom even Solomon. He was wisdom incarnate who in offering to Wisdom's true votaries a deepening knowledge of God, offered their souls forgiveness, peace and tranquility (Mt 11:25-30). If the wisdom of Solomon could express itself in exorcising the demonic, then a "greater than Solomon is here."[2]

The Gathering Storm

Fabled Nineveh had long since entered into history when Jesus began his public ministry within the modest cities by the lake of Galilee. There he wrought "mighty works" or miracles which would credit his proclamation of the kingdom and which, with his teaching, set forth his unique authority. Yet the cities of the lake remained smug and indifferent. They did not repent, until at the last they provoked the anger of Jesus. The language against Chorazin and Bethsaida recalls that of the prophets against Tyre and Sidon as typical of idolatrous and sinful cities.

Tyre and Sidon did not repent but they would have done so, had they been favored to see what the Galilean cities saw when Jesus passed among them (Mt 11:20-22). Inhospitable Sodom for all its perversity will fare better on the day of judgment than Capernaum where the promised light first shone (Mt 4:12-17, 11:23, 24). The tenor of this ominous prophecy is apocalyptic, like thunder signalling the coming storm which was to break upon Israel when the nation rejected its Messiah and provoked divine judgment.

---

[2]E. Lohse, "Solomon," *TDNT* 7 (1971) 463. Cf. the accounts in Jos. *Ant.*, 8, 46–49 and *T. Sol.* 1, 5-7 which tell of Solomon's power over demons. According to Josephus, *Ant.*, 8, 44, one may assume that even in the first century magical books attributed to Solomon were in circulation. D. Duling, "Solomon, Exorcism, and Son of David," *HTR* 68 (1975) 235–252.

Israel Indicted

The Parable of the Two Sons

In his reconstruction of the last week of Jesus' public ministry Matthew recalls in succession three parables accusatory of Israel (Mt 21:28-22:14). The first parable of the two sons is peculiar to Matthew (Mt 21:28-32). In it the leaders of the Jewish nation are accused of affronting the Father in heaven. Though protesting obedience to his will, they do not heed. They remain deaf even to the Baptist and to his prophetic burden. They are thus the second son writ large: the son who in response to his father's command answered, " 'I go, sir,' but did not go" (Mt 21:30). The first son, although he had said that he would not go, afterward repented and went (Mt 21:29). It is he who, the chief priests and elders concede, actually did the will of his father. Thus the leaders of the Jewish nation, the chief priests and elders, bring judgment upon themselves while in a tragic paradox those beyond the pale of the Torah such as tax collectors and prostitutes will enter the kingdom. They acknowledged the word of God and repented (Mt 21:32).

Transfer of the Vineyard

The second of the parables indicts the nation itself (Mt 21:33-43). Israel of old is to fall under a fearful judgment but as a counter-balance to this a new people will emerge in the light of the resurrection (Mt 21:42). Theirs will be the kingdom of God. Commentators have long debated whether the parable as it first appears in Mark (Mk 12:1-12) actually derived from Jesus,[3] or whether it represents reflection of the early church upon the history of salvation with the death of Jesus considered in retrospect.

---

[3]C. H. Dodd, Jeremias, V. Taylor argue that a genuine parable uttered by Jesus himself lies behind the gospel tradition taken up by Mark and then adapted by Matthew and Luke. L. Sabourin, L'Évangile selon Saint Matthieu et ses Principaux Parallèles (Rome: Biblical Institute, 1978) 279. See also M. Boucher, The Parables rev. ed. (Wilmington: Michael Glazier, 1983) that "in recent decades a number of commentators have argued for its authenticity," 155. To C. Carlston, however, following Bultmann and Kümmel, the parable should be ascribed to the church, The Parables of the Triple Tradition (Philadelphia: Fortress, 1975) 181-190.

The parable then becomes a kind of allegory with the tenants standing in for the Israelites, the servants for the prophets, and the son for Jesus.

The role of ancient Israel is at issue. The reference to Israel as the chosen vineyard of the Lord is an old one and at no time more eloquently stated than in Isaiah's Song of the Vineyard (Isa 5:1-7). Now the vineyard becomes the charge of a new people and a new nation which will nurture its fruit. It is the vinedressers of old who will be brought to "a miserable end" (Mt 21:41). It is they, the spiritual leaders of Israel, who ironically pronounce such judgment upon themselves. When they finally conspire for the death of Jesus, the judgment becomes self-fulfilling. The "miserable end" to which they are being brought will transpire in the year 70 admidst the anguish of Jerusalem's fall and the temple's utter destruction. The vineyard will be given to others.

To the parable, Mark and then Matthew and Luke, add reference to the 118th Psalm (Mk 12:10, 11, Lk 20:17, Mt 21:42; Ps 118:22, 23).[4]

> Jesus said to them, "Have you never read in the scriptures: 'The very stone which the builders rejected has become the head of the corner; this was the Lord's doing, and it is marvelous in our eyes'?" (Mt 21:42, Ps 118:22, 23).

The perspective of God cannot be that of man. Though the builders, the proprietors of the Jewish nation and would-be protectors of that heritage, rejected him, Jesus in the wake of his resurrection became the capstone of a new nation, a new community of the elect, the church.[5] And it is charged with providing for the coming harvest (Mt 21:43). To its members will be granted title to the kingdom of God long foreshadowed in the Old Testament. For now consistently with such apocalyptic visionaries as Daniel (Dan 2:44, 7:27), the kingdom is proffered

---

[4]The motif of Jesus Christ as the rejected stone becoming the capstone or keystone of the new structure, that is, the church, is a frequent one in the New Testament. Cf. Acts 4:5-11; 1 Pet 2:4-7; Eph 2:20.

[5]In the gospels, *ekklēsia* appears only in Mt 16:18 and 18:17, and there, as generally in the Septuagint, in the sense of the Hebrew *qahal*, "to call" or "to gather."

to a new people. Jesus offers it with his universal sympathy but at the same time seeks from the new proprietors of the kingdom its appropriate fruits (Mt 7:20). The criterion for adherence to the kingdom is faith: faith issuing in good works and engaging cooperatively in the will of the Father in heaven.

Mensis Caelestis

The theme persists in what is really a fourth parable (Mt 22:11-14) attached to the third parable accusatory of Israel (Mt 22:1-10). There is a criterion for adherence to the kingdom beyond simply acknowledging the invitation. When the kingdom of heaven is compared to a king who gives a marriage feast for his son, then those whom the king will finally receive must be presentable. Be they bad or good when called (Mt 22:10) to recline at the feast, they must be wearing wedding garments, that is, living lives renewed appropriately to the kingdom of heaven "for many are called, but few are chosen" (Mt 22:14).

The third parable accusatory of Israel is actually introduced on a joyful note. "The kingdom of heaven may be compared to a king who gave a marriage feast for his son . . . " (Mt 22:2). A royal wedding possesses a fascination of its own. In the comparable version in Luke's gospel the scene is a great banquet (Lk 14:16-24). The Lukan version is closer to the original but behind the notion of the banquet in both Matthew and Luke lies an ancient and persevering hope. At the last, Isaiah says:

> . . . the Lord of hosts will make for all peoples a feast of fat things, a feast of wine on the lees, of fat things full of marrow, of wine on the lees well refined. And he will destroy on this mountain the covering that is cast over all peoples, the veil that is spread over all nations. He will swallow up death forever, and the Lord God will wipe away tears from all faces, and the reproach of his people he will take away from all the earth; for the Lord has spoken (Isa 25:6-8).

In a nation whose beginnings were forged in the crucible of the desert there persevered the hope of a sumptuous banquet at journey's end. Like the founders and forerunners of their nation the elect of old would one day eat and drink in the presence of God (Ex 24:9-11). With the richness of the Messianic reign, post-exilic Judaism associated, if not that splendid festival beyond the reach of death and sorrow, then at least a fresh abundance attendant to him whose coming signalled the new creation.[6] When those invited to the banquet do not come, then the invitation is extended to "the poor and maimed and blind and lame" (Lk 14:21). The latter represented Jews who had labored under a certain exclusion even from the Temple (Lk 14:23).[7] They are all invited to the banquet. To those invited it would represent the foretaste of heaven.

Matthew in fact enhances the eschatological consideration of the parable. The banquet becomes a marriage feast which the king prepares for his son. Appropriately to the kingdom of heaven a divine invitation is offered the guests. The feast will be consecrated through the divine presence. If it is the king's son who is being honored, who is the bride? In Jewish tradition the people of the old covenant were beloved of the God of Israel. In Ezechiel, chapter sixteen, Psalm forty-five, and especially in the Song of Songs, Israel was the bride of the Lord.[8] In Jewish anticipation of the age to come, God is to renew the marriage bond with his people.[9] The point of the parable is that God would do this but finally through his Son. Servants are dispatched bearing the renewed invitation (Mt 22:3).

The response on the part of those invited was consistent with their history. At one time they had greeted the invitation to renew the covenant with laughter and scorn. This time they simply refused (Mt 22:3). Now everything was ready (Mt 22:4). In the language of Paul it was the fullness of time (Gal 4:4 cf. Eph 1:10). The last days had commenced though their resolution would be

---

[6]Cf. Isa 29:18, 19; 35:5, 6; 61:1; Mt 11:4, 5. For the promised abundance see Pss 81:16; 132:15; 2 Bar 29:4-8. See T. L. Donaldson, *Jesus on the Mountain* (Sheffield, U.K.: JSOT Press, 1985) 126–131.

[7]2 Sam 5:8; 1 QSa 2:5-7.

[8]For the rabbinic tradition describing the sealing of the covenant at Sinai as the marriage of Israel with the Lord see Str-B I 969, II 393.

[9]E. Stauffer, "gameō," *TDNT* 1 (1964) 655.

the more swift for the Israel of the Second Temple; more remote for this age and the world. A second series of messengers is dispatched (Mt 22:4). If the first series recalls the prophets appointed unto Israel, the second could represent Christian "prophets, wise men, and scribes" some of whom were put to death.

Mingled with the blood of the righteous before them, their blood cried to heaven for vengeance. Nor was their crying out finally in vain. "The king was angry, and he sent his troops and destroyed those murderers and burned their city" (Mt 22:7). This dramatic allusion to the judgment visited upon Jerusalem in the year 70 does not appear in Luke's version of the parable. Matthew's redaction, however, probably was written with ashes of the temple in view. In the meantime, the feast stood ready. With royal magnanimity and a sense of forbearance and forgiveness the invitation is extended anew but without apparent discrimination or test. From the highways and byways are gathered both bad and good, the generality of mankind (Mt 22:10).

Protocol Affronted

To the three parables pronouncing judgment upon Israel Matthew adds a fourth, the parable of the wedding garment. Attendance at court demands a certain protocol that cannot be neglected with impunity or go unnoticed by the royal host. When the king himself confronts an insensitive guest, he renders the offender speechless (Mt 22:12). The invitation was gratuitous and ought to have been accepted all the more gratefully, surely not with indifference, neglect, or even contempt.

"Friend, how did you get in here without a wedding garment?" (Mt 22:12). In apocalyptic and intertestamental usage the garment is an image of existence in the age to come, of a life renewed in the new creation. The fabric of life is woven of many strands but unless they consist of words and deeds touched with heavenly grace then that fabric dissolves in the light of divine judgment. For the king is finally God and with divine prerogative sentences the offender to the outer darkness. "For many are called, but few are chosen" (Mt 22:14). The judgment thus threatened Gentile Christians is reminiscent of that promised Jewry in a similar context. Jesus had promised the nations at large an invitation to the heavenly festival graced by the patriarchs and prophets and by the divine presence, while at the same time he warned Israel of its rejection (Mt 8:11, 12; cf. Lk 13:28, 30). Now the nations have been invited. Let them receive the invitation gratefully, with neither exaggerated fear nor presumption. How they receive the invitation will afford a criterion for judgment.

Enthusiasm

The church whence Matthew wrote was troubled by false teachers (Mt 5:17-20, 7:15-27, 24:10-12). It is hardly conceivable that they would have rejected whole and entire "the law and the prophets." They were enthusiasts and while setting forth the gospel in the first flush of the resurrection at a time so richly spiritual they might well have disparaged the old. Yet, "every scribe who has been trained for the kingdom of heaven is like a householder who brings out of his treasure what is new and what is old" (Mt 13:52). The false prophets would not have understood that while the cleavage between the old and the new, signalled by the resurrection of Jesus, was deep beyond all human assessment, the cleavage was far less between Christianity and the tradition of ancient Israel, between Jesus and the prophets before him, than between the new humanity revealed in the risen Lord and the old mankind laboring under sentence of sin and death. Thus false teachers would have disparaged the old all round. Others were perplexed that the prophets of old could appear to have spoken in vain, or that the law, revered as the oracle of God, could be utterly abrogated.

The new creation heralded by Jesus Christ would indeed be far removed from the old. To the degree that it is not yet realized, there remains a continuity not only with the old, that is the age that is passing with its bondage to sin and death, but with the law and the prophets, their promise and hope conveyed. The resolute assertion of Jesus that he had come not to abolish the law and the prophets but to fulfill them (Mt 5:17) may have found incentive to its recollection in the very community whence Matthew wrote. The fulfillment would imply as exacting an imperative as that of the law and the prophets themselves (cf. Ps 1:1, 2; Josh 1:8). Were some teaching otherwise? (Mt 5:19).

At the conclusion of the Sermon on the Mount, a certain presumption of the enthusiasts is the more sharply addressed "On that day many will say to me, 'Lord, Lord, did we not prophesy in your name, and cast out demons in your name, and do many mighty works in your name?' And then I will declare to them, 'I never knew you; depart from me, you evildoers' " (Mt 7:22, 23). At the final assize those who had presumed upon grace will answer to the source of all grace. The criterion of judgment shall remain, reverence and obedience to our father in heaven (Mt 7:21). Jesus progressed to Jerusalem and the Cross in utter fidelity to the will of his father. In this fidelity unto death Jesus expressed the substance and bond of the new covenant between God and man, even as obedience to the law and the prophets had confirmed the old.

Prospect of Judgment

False prophets are mentioned also in Jesus' discourse on the end of the age (Mt 24:11). Christians are warned of confusion and betrayal within the church while "lawlessness" or sin will prevail without. Before the workers of evil (Mt 7:23, 13:41) looms the day of judgment. Among the synoptics Matthew's vocabulary contains a preponderantly large number of words and expressions which are associated with judgment. Only Matthew contains detailed descriptions of the last judgment (Mt 7:21ff., 13:36ff., 25:31ff.). It is not the mortal prospect common to a fallen race which is emphasized in the first canonical gospel, that prospect can be relieved through bringing forth "fruits of repentance." It is rather that the evangelist insists on the retribution due the words and deeds of individual men and women (Mt 12:36, 16:27). Reward or punishment will be meted out at the last judgment according to what one has said or done. Each man and woman will be held to account for their works (Mt 16:27) and for their words (Mt 12:36). Matthew makes clear that when sincerely discharged the three-fold offices of religion: almsgiving, prayer, and fasting, will be rewarded (Mt 6:1-17). So too will be rewarded the merciful, the peacemakers, the single-hearted, and all who quest for greater righteousness (Mt 5:3-12). Yet the threat of punishment also looms large in Matthew and it is significant that Matthew speaks of reward and punishment chiefly in eschatological terms: the kingdom or the outer darkness: heaven or hell. To him especially, gehenna is a place of outer darkness where "men will weep and gnash their teeth."

Beyond Due Measure

In Matthew reward can be cast in terms of greater compensation than appropriate to the work itself. While God is a just God, no less attributable to him are magnanimity and mercy. Matthew's reference to compensation is made in the light of heaven and eternity. An eschatological law of talion seems at work. Because it is eschatological, that is, ordered to the age to come, it will be resolved through divine corroboration and for eternity. The ancient Mosaic law of talion as existent among men and constraining to a strict *quid pro quo* is superseded.

If the traditional acts of religion are truly religious or oriented to God rather than to man, then their reward shall be appropriately divine (Mt 6:1-17). If they are not truly religious but aspire to the passing applause of men, then that applause will be sufficient recompense even to would-be men of God. To true men of God, prophets and the righteous, for reasons that they are such, theirs also will be the reward which crowns prophecy and righteousness, the comprehension of divine light and love (Mt 10:41, cf. I Cor 13:12).

Laborers in the Vineyard: Early and Late

In the parable of the laborers in the vineyard the evangelist brings out the generosity that characterizes divine recompense (Mt 20:1-16). It is unique to Matthew. The *dramatis personae* consist of a householder or owner of the vineyard and the laborers; some are hired to work through the long day, others, for a few hours, and finally, those hired at the eleventh hour to work only one hour. The kingdom of heaven is likened to an owner of a vineyard and his hiring of laborers (Mt 20:1). But the real point of the parable is the reckoning of the owner with the laborers. His is a generous reckoning. To those hired at the eleventh hour and who could therefore labor in the vineyard but one hour, the owner offers a day's pay or the same amount rendered those who were first hired and who labored all day. It was not as though the recompense was insufficient for those who labored all day long. They received what was their due in justice, a *quid pro quo*. Were those who were hired at the eleventh hour to receive only what was due for one hour's work, they would be justly compensated but hardly sufficiently. Here then justice looks to magnanimity and mercy to enhance compensation and reward.

Even so, those who were paid justly and sufficiently for their day's work grumbled at their owner's generosity. They were displeased at the owner of the vineyard and displeased with their fellow laborers that having achieved and merited so little, they could receive such largesse. God's ways are simply not our ways where man can hope for no more than what he has earned. The parable would relate the reckoning of service to the kingdom of heaven. In so doing it translates the reckoning into a sphere beyond human understanding. Only in faith can man acknowledge the divine largesse which would admit harlot and tax collector to the kingdom of God even before those charged in Israel's latter days with preserving the religious sentiment of the nation (Mt 21:28-32). They had been so charged early on, but in vain. For the sake of their human tradition they made void the word of God (Mt 15:6). The prostitutes and revenue agents were called late but they answered in faith the preaching of the Baptist and Jesus Christ, "Repent, for the kingdom of heaven is at hand" (Mt 3:2, 4:17). They brought forth fruits befitting repentance and they gleaned for the Lord of the harvest a pleasing vintage. Thus, the new criterion by which all shall be rewarded or punished. Did they bring forth fruit appropriate to repentance? Did they suffer that change of heart by which a man or woman is oriented to the kingdom? Or, rather were they left to wander in the primordial darkness? Every man and woman will answer for their words and works (Mt 16:27) though their words and deeds constitute only the vesture with which the inner, true self is clothed and defined: a vessel of election or of wrath.

The parable of the laborers in the vineyard in the first instance was probably addressed to those critical of Jesus, that he preached hope to sinners. Judaism did not deny the possibility of repentance. Yet in its latter days Judaism emphasized the advantage of works as much, if not more than faith; merit, more than God's gratuitous grace which is the source of our justification (cf. e.g. Rom 9:30-33). One can compare a rabbinic parallel of a later day when the subject receives a whole day's salary although he worked only two hours. Yet in those two hours he did more than anyone else could do in an entire day. Hence he is rewarded on the basis of what he had done.

God will not be constrained in his magnanimity or mercy to whosoever finally answers his call. Only faith could lead to the enlargement of Judaism's crimped perspective: faith and Jesus Christ who in plumbing the divine abyss becomes the true exponent of the law and the prophets. "For who has known the mind of the Lord, or who has been his counsellor?" (Rom 11:34; cf. Isa 40:13).

3

The Passing of Jerusalem
and of the World

Quomodo sedet sola civitas . . . (Lam 1:1)

The death of King Agrippa I in 44 A.D. signalled a decline in public order and in that decline the sages of Israel perceived omens of the coming disaster. The great rabbi Johanan ben Zakkai who was said to have taken over from Hillel and Shammai voiced his warnings. One rabbinic tradition had the rabbi Zadok fasting about 30 A.D. to forestall the destruction of Jerusalem. Jesus' own lament over the holy city was resonant of the baleful prophecies of Micah and Jeremiah before an earlier Jerusalem and the first temple (Jer 26:9, 18; cf. Mic 3:12). The temple in the time of Jesus had stood for over five hundred years since the earlier judgment reduced it to ashes and seared the conscience of the nation. In 586 B.C. the nation answered for its idolatry and the crimes of a long line of kings "who did evil in the eyes of the Lord and walked not in the ways of their father David." During the long reign of Manasseh the doom of the nation had been sealed. Prophets had voiced their warning (2 Kgs 21:10-16; cf. Jer 22:5) even as Jesus voiced his warnings to a generation which had scorned his emissaries (Mt 23:34-36) and would crucify him. Amid the darkening shadows of his nation's twilight Jesus evokes with clairvoyance the spectre of the ruined temple. ". . . There will not be left here one stone upon another, that will not be thrown down" (Mt 24:2).

The ominous sentence appears in one form or another in the four gospels. That Jesus could be the new temple through whom not only men but also women, not only Jew but also Gentile could approach God, his enemies would not concede. His warnings, nevertheless, about the passing of the old order and the destruction of the temple were recalled at his trial and crucifixion (Mt 26:61, 27:40; cf. Mk 14:58, 15:29). The warning appropriately follows Jesus' vain and tragic appeal to Jerusalem (Mt 23:37-39). It follows the long indictment of the scribes and the Pharisees which encompasses the twenty-third chapter of Matthew.

At the same time the text introduces the extended discourse of Jesus upon the fall of the temple and Jerusalem and upon the end of the world. In the first canonical gospel, chapters twenty-four and twenty-five represent the fifth extended discourse. Like the four preceding, it is a composite work. Chapter twenty-four of Matthew follows Mark 13 though subtracting some and adding some from the Q source common to Matthew and Luke and from a source consistent with a uniquely Matthean tradition.

The old order was passing. The nation Israel would shortly answer for the rejection of Christ and the mockery of his emissaries. They would answer for the blood of the righteous, even that of Christ (Mt 23:34, 27:25). ". . . God's wrath had come upon them at last," Paul had written to the Christians at Thessalonica early on (1 Thess 2:16). The death of the king Agrippa I in 44, the ill-fated insurrection of Theudas in 44-46, the famine of 46-47, the expulsion of the Jews from Rome by the Emperor Claudius in 49-50, all seemed to reflect the brooding wrath.[1] But the end was not yet, neither of the temple nor of this age. Strife among nations, famine and earthquakes will occur. Though the litany of such calamities is common enough to the apocalyptic genre they are in truth part of history and in these latter days all the more dramatic. In the view of the evangelist they now represent the beginnings, the birth pangs or travail which characterizes the new order as it emerges amidst the old (Mt 24:8).[2]

---

[1]B. Rigaux, *Saint Paul: Les Épitres aux Thessaloniciens* (Paris: Gabalda, 1956) 454; L. Gaston, *No Stone on another: Studies in the Significance of the Fall of Jerusalem in the synoptic Gospels* (Leiden: Brill, 1970) 463-468.

[2]Again, an apocalyptic motif: Zeph 1:3; 4 Esdras 5:7, 6:14-18, 21-24; Apoc. Bar 27, 48:31-37, 70:2-10; Sib. Or. 3:796. See Str-B 4, 977ff..

The emergence of the new order or the kingdom of God cannot be without anguish. In these last words of Jesus to his disciples before his passion, death, and resurrection, he speaks of their coming trial and peril of execution. This he does in the context of the last days, both of the temple and the world. The end is as the beginning. Trial and persecution stalk the vanguard of the Messianic kingdom. Persecution of the Christians had already begun at Matthew's writing and it may be that recollection of the words of Jesus had been colored by the experience of some Christians. At the same time the evangelist expresses his great anxiety about apostasy within the Christian community. For the second time in this, Jesus' last extended discourse, the warning is set forth of false prophets (Mt 24:5, 11), prophets upon whom the damning sentence was pronounced in the course of Jesus' first discourse, the Sermon on the Mount (Mt 7:21-23). Yet amid the anguish of these last days, of the temple and Jerusalem, and then of the world, the disciples of Jesus must persevere (Mt 24:13). Only when the gospel is preached throughout the world will the end come (Mt 24:14).

The judgment is at hand. Upon the Holy City it had already come when the evangelist recalls Jesus' warnings in vivid and apocalyptic colors. Jesus' last discourse had begun with his prophecy uttered above Jerusalem that no stone would be left upon another. The vision of the temple whose marble mass was so long espied from afar like a snowy mount fretted with pinnacles of gold, was to be dissolved. And this amidst such anguish "as had not been from the beginning of the world" (Mt 24:21). The temple and Jerusalem were dissolved in the blood of their defenders. The fearful cry raised by the people at the arraignment of Jesus before Pontius Pilate, "His blood be on us and on our children" (Mt 27:25) is answered. The judgment executed.

The End of the World

To the reduction of the temple and Jerusalem will succeed the end of this passing age, the dissolution of the world in its present form.[3] That is the faith evoked through Jesus Christ. It is as though the former signals the latter, a last and universal judgment (Mt 25:32). For all that its day and hour is unknown, Matthew teaches through the parable of the fig tree that the Lord is near—"at the very gates" (Mt 24:33). Yet false prophets and false Messiahs will arise. For the third time the elect are warned to be wary of being led astray. Self-anointed Messiahs and false prophets may work even "great signs and wonders" (Mt 24:24), but if they do so they will do so in the service of error. They may speak in the wilderness or speak in the city and be silenced only at the last. Let followers of Christ beware. The immediate prelude to the Second Coming will be awful to behold. "For as the lightning comes from the east and shines as far as the west, so will be the coming of the Son of Man" (Mt 24:27). Though he will come as deliverer of the church, he will also come as judge of men and nations.

Prior to his description of the last judgment Matthew sets forth a series of five parables: those of the fig tree, Noah, the evil servant, the ten virgins, and the talents. Uncertainty about the precise time and yet certainty as to the fact of the coming judgment characterizes at least the latter four parables.

Watch and Pray!
The Fig Tree as Herald of Summer

Though the parable follows immediately upon an apocalyptic vision of the world's end (Mt 24:29-31) and though its own sense of urgency is augmented by the reiterated warning of universal disintegration (Mt 24:35), yet the parable is essentially hopeful.[4] Summer is near when the fig tree sprouts forth its green and leafy

---

[3]Cf. 1 Cor 7:31. Here in chapter 24 the evangelist expressed a similarly apocalyptic vision.

[4]C. Carlston, *The Parables* 197, "Of this parable we can say with some assurance only that it arose in a Palestinian milieu—the agriculture is really only comprehensible there—and that it is used by Mark to strengthen and console his readers. That he chose to embed this parable in a chapter of marked apocalyptic outlook shows how seriously he took persecution and suffering as not beyond the knowledge and grace of God. The true *telos* of the Christian is not cosmic desolation but hope." See also J. Jeremias, *The Parables of Jesus* (2nd ed.; New York: Scribner's, 1970) 119, 120.

vesture. The tree is transformed from a death-like appearance to life, signalling the coming of summer. The harvest is not emphasized. But the close of the age and the Lord's sure reckoning with humanity will feature the parables following. Here in this lovely parable Jesus evokes the season of light, life, and warmth. No less dramatic and no less certain will be his second coming to dispel forever from the community of man the darkness of sin and the chill of death. He already stands at the gate (Mt 24:33). Though the stars should fall and the constellations crumble in the promised metamorphosis of this paradise lost, the word of the Lord shall endure (Mt 24:35). In that word lies our hope.

Through the introduction of verse 34, a particular urgency attaches to the argument that this generation will not pass away until all these things take place. The reference to "this generation" is perplexing. But it can enhance the paraenetic and minatory slant of this and the succeeding parables. The verse was perhaps introduced into the present context (Mt 24:32-35) with this in mind. What was the actual situation to which Jesus sought to convey a sense of urgency cannot be ascertained, so much the more so since a similar sentiment appears in a different context: namely, the missionary discourse (Mt 10:23). Jesus could have spoken the words in reference to his coming death and resurrection.[5] For therein would transpire the turning of the ages: his signal victory over sin and death was the beginning of the end to an age long in thrall to our ancient enemies. "All was being accomplished" (Mt 24:34, 5:18). When Matthew recalls the words of Jesus in his discourse on the destruction of Jerusalem and the end of the world, the evangelist is addressing his own generation or rather, the church. He does so with the thought that the end of the present age has already been set in motion. The ruins of the temple and of Jerusalem could not but have haunted him and brought home to him as to every Jew the transience of all things. Indeed, "Heaven and earth will pass away, but my words will not pass away" (Mt. 24:35). Though in time they would pray, *pro mora finis,* to delay the end, in the beginning Christians prayed that the Lord would come and come swiftly (1 Thess 4:16,

---

[5]Meier, *Matthew* 172.

1 Cor 16:22). Verse 34, however, ought not really be adduced to suggest the imminence of the Second Coming. On the contrary, in the following parables great emphasis is laid upon the uncertainty of the final hour[6] and on the long delay of the Second Coming.

"But of that day and hour no none knows. . ."

The whole point of the parable which follows next in Jesus' discourse on the end of the age is the uncertainty of its timing. The end will come suddenly and without warning like the irruption of a tidal wave which once mounted inundates all within its long and irreversible reach. As though there were at work that blind but sure fate so feared by the ancients, at the final catastrophe one will be taken and one will be left (Mt 24:40, 41). The figure for all this is the primeval flood. The terror of the deluge is not what is being emphasized—it is unwary and uncertain man, with little faith, who goes about his eating and drinking, marrying and giving in marriage, while beneath the surface calm the depths are in convulsion. But as it was in the days of Noah, so will it be at the coming of the Son of Man (Mt 24:37).

Again, it is not the judgment with its irrevocable decree of reward or punishment which the evangelist would emphasize here, it is its uncertain timing. The promise of reward or threat of punishment will be featured in the parables which follow (Mt 24:45-25:30). Here, unlike Luke who is following Q, Matthew does not enhance the note of judgment inherent in the deluge by then referring to the fire and brimstone rained down upon the cities of the plain.[7] For this parable it is enough to teach that the time of the ultimate assize is unknown. At the beginning of Jesus' discourse on the end of the age the disciples had asked him, ". . . What will be the sign of your coming and of the close of the age?" (Mt 24:3). Jesus offered signs. They can indicate that like the des-

---

[6]Strecker, *Der Weg der Gerechtigkeit* 43.

[7]Lk 17:28, 29; cf. 2 Pet 2:5-7. Fitzmyer ascribes the reference to the judgment on Sodom to Luke's own source. J. Fitzmyer, *The Gospel according to Luke X-XXIV* (Garden City, New York: Doubleday, 1985) 1165 (Anchor Bible 28A).

truction of Jerusalem the end of the present age is approaching. Beyond that the signs remain inconclusive even to the clairvoyant. The church cannot know when her Lord shall return (Mt 24:42). Nor do the angels in heaven know. And Jesus himself forbears plumbing the divine abyss (Mt 24:36).

It is enough to know that the age to come dawned on Calvary, on the morning of the resurrection, and at Pentecost. At the same time, the world, the present age, was judged. The moral which the evangelist draws for the church is clear: The end is coming. Watch and pray! To reinforce his argument Matthew adds, (probably from Q, though there in a different context) the common metaphor of the thief. To achieve his purpose, the thief comes without notice and at night. So will be the coming of the Son of Man—without notice. Christians must stand in readiness (Mt 24:44) through dynamic belief.

In the more extended parables which follow, this theme perseveres (Mt 24:43–25:30): We know neither the day nor the hour of the Second Coming. But in the parables, the evil servant, the ten maidens, and the talents, judgment is emphasized. Though the parousia of the Lord is delayed, that delay ought not be the occasion for indifference, sloth, and relapse into the ways of the old mankind.

Stewardship

The parable of the servant revolves about the stewardship or management of a great house. Here Matthew and Luke follow Q yet the Matthean redaction especially weights the parable toward its otherworldly dimension (Mt 24:51). The servant may be faithful to his charge or he may not. In the latter case in Luke's version he is judged faithless (Lk 12:46). According to Matthew he is damned. Actually the judgment in Luke is tantamount to the destruction of the evil servant, but in Matthew his typical imagery of rage and utter destruction is evoked as the lot of the damned. This is no ordinary house to which the parable points. It is the church which lies under the charge of the servants of the Lord. If they are servants faithful to the Lord, then they will be blessed (Mt 24:45); but if they are faithless, when the master does return and the day of reckoning arrives, then the faithless servant will fare no better than did the hypocrites whose charge was Israel of old (Mt 24:51; cf. Mt 23). That the evil servant beat his fellow servants bespeaks arrogance and impatience. Perhaps his want of patience was of a deeper sort. He eats and drinks with his drunken fellows (Mt 24:49). Patience[8] characterizes the true servant of the Lord not only amidst trial and persecution in the beginning (Mt 10:22) and in the end (Mt 24:13), but in the slowly evolving centuries, even millennia, which must precede the Second Coming. Without patience is hope other than illusory? Without hope will not men yield to the hedonism born of despair? Such was the fate of the evil servant who in acquiescing to despair in this life, acquiesced for eternity (Mt 24:51). This, although in the years intervening between his passage among us and his second coming as judge, Jesus is yet with the church. "Lo, I am with you always, to the close of the age" (Mt 28:20). To those who seek, with Jesus can be found forgiveness.

The Second Coming and its deferral remains the issue. The second extended parable revolving about the judgment was drawn from contemporary wedding customs. The realistic description set forth in Matthew could find some parallel as late as Palestinian wedding customs under the Ottoman empire.[9] The wedding festival itself would be at night. The bridegroom would be met with flaming lamps and then accompanied by the torch bearers to the bride and to the wedding itself. The bridegroom would often be delayed in approaching the bride if for no other reason than to offer appropriate presents to the bride's family. In this parable all the maidens should have made themselves ready to meet the bridegroom and to accompany him to the nuptial rites. But five of the ten were foolish and did not make ready. At least they did

---

[8]upomonē, cf. Mt 10:22, 24:13, a steadfast and patient endurance deriving from Christian faith and especially hope. See F. Hauck, " 'upomenō, 'upomonē," *TDNT* 4 (1967) 581–588.

[9]Jeremias, *The Parables* 171–175, Boucher, *The Parables* 134–138. But see D. Via, that in view of our imprecise knowledge of Palestinian wedding practices, various possible wedding customs could have been brought together to serve the narrative purpose of Jesus. D. Via, *The Parables: Their Literary and Existential Dimension* (Philadelphia: Fortress, 1967) 124.

not prepare for the possibility that the groom's coming would be delayed. So when the groom does come the foolish maidens are not ready to accompany him. They are excluded from the wedding to which they had been invited. What ought to have brought great joy to the maidens turned out to be a great disappointment.

While there is no reference in the Old Testament or in the rabbinic and intertestamental literature to the Messiah as bridegroom, what is at issue here in the first instance is the divine visitation embodied in Jesus. As in the earlier parable of the heavenly banquet, all are invited: the good and the bad, the wise and the foolish, humanity in general. But the foolish are finally rejected, just as is the man without the wedding garment. On both occasions the rejection was a shock to human complacency and smugness, the shattering effect of a crisis which unmasks us as unprepared and strips us of our easy optimism.[10]

That Matthew in transmitting the parable should have interpreted the divine visitation as the judgment actually enhances the summons to watchfulness and readiness already inherent in the narrative. The concluding admonition, "Watch, therefore, for you know neither the day nor the hour" (Mt 25:13), may not have been integral to the original parable, but the sentiment is surely appropriate to its main thrust even though the maidens themselves slept until the coming of the bridegroom. The wise at least were ready for his coming.

Before the foolish the door to the festival or to the heavenly repast is closed. This is an important theme in Matthew.[11] In the last days Jesus will stand at the door (Mt 24:33) and admit those properly prepared (Mt 25:10, 21, 23). That entrance through the door is not easy was stressed in the Sermon on the Mount, "Enter by the narrow gate; for the gate is wide and the way is easy, that leads to destruction, and those who enter by it are many. For the gate is narrow and the way is hard, that leads to life, and those who find it are few" (Mt 7:13, 14). It is precisely because entrance through the door involves doing the will of the Father that Matthew is so critical of the false piety (Mt 6:5, 6) represented by the

[10]Cf. ibid. 126.

[11]K. Donfried, "Allegory of the Ten Virgins," *JBL* 93 (1974) 422, 423.

Pharisees: "But woe to you scribes and Pharisees, hypocrites! because you shut the kingdom of heaven against men; for you neither enter yourselves, nor allow those who would enter to go in" (Mt 23:13). To the foolish the door to the wedding banquet is closed. Thus they are separated from the blessed in Matthew's vivid description of the last judgment (Mt 25:31-46).

No Security: No Risk

The evangelist sets forth one further parable before concluding Jesus' discourse on the end of Jerusalem and on the end of the world. That is the parable of the talents. A man about to go on a long journey entrusts considerable amounts of money ranging from one to five talents to his servants. One talent at that time was tantamount to a laborer's wages for fifteen years. Evidently, if invested, it could command considerable in return by way of interest on the principal. But the servant who received the one talent buried it. He was anxious and afraid even in the face of what apparently could have been a sound investment. The servants who received two talents or five talents managed to double the principal during their master's absence. But the servant who received the one talent would not take any risk at all. He was anxious and afraid.

From this parable the word talent entered the English language to mean a natural endowment or gift. In the context of the early church, talents could encompass even charismata or supernatural gifts. For all the surpassing advantage of the latter to the swift diffusion of nascent Christianity they could on occasion be exploited to the disadvantage of the church. That would be because they were possessed by enthusiasts. This parable concerns rather the anxious and fearful, those to whom to possess a singular talent would be inconvenient or too risky to develop. Though Matthew could be thought to be adapting the parable to the early church and especially to its leaders, more likely he had in mind the generality of Christians. Jesus had first spoken the parable perhaps having latter-day Judaism in mind. Though called to be a priestly people and to mediate among the pagans their singular vision of God and his law, the Jews failed. If they did not bury, they at least fenced in the Torah and judged the *goyyim* sinners. Or Jesus may have had in mind the scribes and the Pharisees, Judaism's spiritual leaders. Thanks to their scrupulosity and severity "the weightier matters of the law" were all but eclipsed in the eyes of the people (Mt 23:23). When the evangelist adapts the parable to his church he addresses not only the leaders but the followers of Jesus generally.

The first of the last three extended parables revolving about the Second Coming and the judgment does indeed appear to have been addressed to church leaders. Servants of the Lord, they shall render an account at his coming (Mt 24:45-51). In the second parable, that of the wise or foolish maidens, men could see in that distinction something typical of humanity in general, wise or foolish, good or bad. When invited to the wedding, like the man who had no wedding garment (Mt 22:11), the foolish maidens would not prepare themselves. The door to the festival is closed and the threshold barred to their access. It is in the last parable of the brief series that the judgment is proposed the most severely and that from an otherwordly perspective: "And cast the worthless servant into the outer darkness; there men will weep and gnash their teeth" (Mt 25:30). This dramatic portrait of irredeemable despair is that of the evangelist and balances the joy of the Lord to which good and faithful servants are admitted (Mt 25:21, 23).

The parable is adapted differently in Matthew and Luke (Lk 19:11-27). Matthew is probably closer to the original but the emphasis on judgment issuing in joy or banishment to the outer darkness is that of the evangelist. Similarly Matthean is the accolade afforded the servants who doubled their master's principal. They were good and according to Matthew, "faithful" servants (Mt 25:21, 23; cf. Lk 19:17). It was the servant who received one talent who, anxious and afraid, would take no risk. He was of little faith like those whom Jesus chided in the Sermon on the Mount for not trusting in their heavenly Father (Mt 6:30).[12] He could not venture beyond himself because he was unsure of the ground whereon he stood. Only the man of faith standing on a transcendent and immovable ground can venture all in the face of the

[12]Cf. Mt 8:26, 14:31, 16:8.

unknown.[13] The parable, especially in the light of the Matthean redaction emphasizing the servants' accountability and their punishment or reward, prepares for the great and terrible scene which follows: the Last Judgment.

The Last Judgment

"My Lord, what a morning, when the stars begin to fall . . ."

All the tribes of the earth will mourn even as the elect are summoned to share the victory of the Son of Man (Mt 24:30, 31). The universe will be reduced to chaos and against the ensuing darkness he will appear. Darkness had enshrouded the earth at the death of Jesus. The veil of the temple was rent; the earth quaked; and the bodies of the saints were raised (Mt 27:51-53). Thus was signalled in the mind of the evangelist the passing of an age in thrall to sin and death. Amid such shaking of its foundation the present age could even then espy the still tremulous lightning and hear the distant thunder which presages its coming end. A cosmic storm was brewing to precede the Second Coming. "Truly this was the Son of God!" acknowledged the centurion and his company when they saw the earthquake and what took place at the death of Jesus (Mt 27:54). First to acknowledge the redemption was this Gentile. And since that supreme hour in human history how many have fallen asleep in the Lord to await the last trumpet! (Mt 24:31). Yet at the last the tribes of the earth will mourn. This world and this passing age will mourn with fear and without hope as it faces its demise.

At the last and universal judgment of men and nations some will go away into eternal punishment, but the righteous into eternal life (Mt 25:46). Among the evangelists this vision of the judgment was Matthew's alone. Against the background of a crumbling world the blessed on the one hand and the damned on the other are finally distinguished. He who alone was privy to what had been hidden since the foundation of the world (Mt 13:35) will now summon the blessed beyond the dissolving ramparts of

[13]Cf. Via, *The Parables* 120, 121.

this world to the kingdom prepared for them since the foundation of the world. The damned will be denied the kingdom and sentenced to the keep of the devil and his angels (Mt 25:41). What is the criterion by which judgment is rendered? It is rendered on the basis of how one has responded to the imperative of love.

With this vision of the last judgment the evangelist concludes Jesus' last extended discourse. As in Jesus' first discourse, the Sermon on the Mount, where his fulfillment and reinterpretation of the law and the prophets crystallized finally in the Golden Rule, so here is emphasized the primacy of love in reference even to the least of Jesus' brothers and sisters (Mt 25:40).

The Least of the Brethren

Who actually are to be judged is debated among commentators. That "all nations" should be summoned to the last assize (Mt 25:32) suggests that all men and women will answer on that day for their disposition to the poor and dispossessed, the least of the brethren. Jesus identifies himself with those who hunger and thirst, with strangers and even the imprisoned. In the first instance Jesus identifies himself with his disciples or his "little ones" (Mt 10:40-42, 18:6; cf. 28:20). In their hunger and thirst, their weakness and lowliness, in their persecutions Jesus is with them. "He who receives you," Jesus had said to his disciples in the missionary discourse, "receives me, and he who receives me receives him who sent me" (Mt 10:40). In the hunger and thirst of his disciples, in their weakness and suffering the features of the Crucified are revealed. A dynamism whose source is divine appears at the same time. Paul speaks eloquently in his second letter to the Corinthians of the dialectic at work within Christian existence, the dialectic between weakness, dying and death on the one hand and divine power and resurrection on the other (2 Cor 4:7, 10, 11). Matthew also sets forth a dialectic between weakness and power.[14]

---

[14]Mt 10:16-23, especially vv 19 and 20; also, Mt 12:17-21, 21:4-17. See John R. Donahue, "The 'Parable' of the Sheep and the Goats: A Challenge to Christian Ethics," *TS* 47 (1986) 25-28.

It is Jesus who first proceeds in weakness and suffering and finally death, that thereby he might save his people from their sins (Mt 1:21). But a disciple is not above his teacher nor a servant above his master. Paradoxically it is in the weakness and suffering of Jesus' disciples, in their willingness to engage in the mystery of the Cross that the kingdom of God is advanced. It would seem no mere coincidence then that from Matthew's perspective the parable of the sheep and the goats should precede the account of the passion of Jesus and his embrace of the bitter cross.

Compassion and Consecration

On the Cross and crucified between thieves, Jesus revealed his deepest solidarity with all sinners, men and women alike. He dies on the Cross. So not only his disciples but all who hunger and thirst, who are weak and suffer, and finally die, will bear the features of the Crucified. To them especially Christians ought to extend what love requires. The sated and powerful of this world may contemn them but at peril of damnation. Even long before Christ, suffering was thought somehow to consecrate and hallow.[15] In Israel the Hebrew word *'anawim* meant the poor and afflicted who persevered in the expectation that the Lord would vindicate them (cf. Isa 49:13, 61:1, 2). They were thought to be the special charge of heaven. Although Jewish lists of good works did not include visiting prisoners, they did include ministry to the hungry, the thirsty, and the sick, clothing the naked and welcoming strangers.[16]

---

[15]A theme often voiced by the chorus in the Greek tragedy. For the treatment generally, see Sophocles' *Oedipus at Colonnus.*

[16]Jeremias, *The Parables* 207.

4

The Savior

In his death on the cross Jesus achieves utter solidarity with man. He becomes the true mediator between God and man, sealing with his blood a new covenant which offers forgiveness of sin and hope in the face of judgment. The expiatory advantage of Christ's sacrifice had long been understood in the early church. In his letter to the Romans, Paul adapts even earlier testimony to the mystery (Rom 3:21-26). Later the author of the letter to the Hebrews will write of the blood "that speaks more graciously than the blood of Abel" (Heb 12:24). For the blood of Christ as expiatory, and propitiatory, summons divine forgiveness, not vengeance. Among the evangelists it is in Matthew's account that the blood of the covenant is said to be "poured out for many *unto the forgiveness of sins"* (Mt 26:28).

In the late New Testament letter to the Hebrews, the mystery is broached substantially and thematically. Significantly, reference to Jeremiah (31:31-34) introduces and closes the crowning argument of that letter that "without the shedding of blood there is no forgiveness" (Heb 9:22) and that Christ "appeared once for all at the end of the age to put away sin by the sacrifice of himself" (Heb 9:27). In Christ is the hopeful and moving prophecy of Jeremiah fulfilled.

> "Behold, the days are coming, says the Lord, when I will make a new covenant with the house of Israel and the house of Judah, not like the covenant which I made with their fathers, when I took them by the hand to bring them out of the land of Egypt, my covenant which they broke, though I was their husband,

says the Lord. But this is the covenant which I will make with the house of Israel after those days, says the Lord: I will put my law within them, and I will write it upon their hearts: and I will be their God, and they shall be my people. And no longer shall each man teach his brother, saying, 'Know the Lord,' for they shall all know me, from the least of them to the greatest, says the Lord; for I will forgive their iniquity, and I will remember their sin no more" (Jeremiah 31:31-34).

The words of Jesus at the last supper after the Matthean redaction are surely resonant with the hope voiced by the prophet long before. That the prophecy is being fulfilled underscores the eschatological and otherworldly dimensions of the words of Jesus. They are consistent with the promise to the sons of Zebedee that "the Son of Man came not to be served but to serve, and to give his life as a ransom for many" (Mt 20:28, Mk 10:45, cf. Isa 53). Jeremiah voiced his hope at a tragic watershed in his nation's history. The nation was being judged. The temple was in ruins and Jerusalem lay desolate. The people languished in exile. Yet at the word of the prophet they revive.

The revival, however, would not be all that the people hoped. Though delivered from Babylon, the nation continued to labor under alien kings: Persian, Greek, and finally Roman. Against that shifting and somber background, the Maccabean revolt (175-135) and the Hasmonean succession (145-63) was as brief as it was brilliant. The temple was rebuilt but neither as men remembered it nor as they envisioned it (Hag 2:3). Its embellishment would be the work of generations.

In those same generations of the post-exilic period, Yom Kippur or the "Day of Expiation" would loom especially significant. Expiatory sacrifice had always existed in Israel but it became much more important when a national crisis such as the Babylonian exile or later, oppression by the Seleucid king, Antiochus IV, brought home to the people a deepened sense of their own sin and guilt.[1] At the same time increased devotion to the Torah made much more serious the infraction of it and the ensuing guilt.

[1]R. deVaux, *Ancient Israel: Its Life and Institutions* (tr. John McHugh; New York: McGraw-Hill, 1961) 453, 454.

Coincidentally with renewed attention to cult, the priesthood itself was magnified in the person of the high priest,[2] especially on the day of atonement. "How glorious he was when the people gathered round him as he came out of the inner sanctuary" (Sir 50:5). The advantage of the high priest's sacrifice of goats and bulls unto the expiation of sin would pale utterly beside the surpassing advantage of Christ's sacrifice (Heb 9:13-14). For it is through his blood that sin is expiated, the sinner forgiven, and hope afforded in the face of judgment. Of Jesus would be predicated the sprinkled blood that speaks more graciously than the blood of Abel (Heb 12:24). Is not forgiveness the singular blessing inherent in the new covenant foretold by Jeremiah and inaugurated by Jesus Christ at the dawn of the new age? He came to save us from our sins (Mt 1:21).

Jesus: Our Savior

Among the Jews would salvation dawn and only after that, among the nations at large. Joseph is to call the name of the child "Jesus," "for he will save his people from their sins" (Mt 1:21). The name derives from the root of a Hebrew word meaning "God helps." Thus Joshua who succeeded Moses and led his people into the promised land, bore the name whose root meaning was "God's help." Jesus' name is actually derived from a shortened form of the same Hebrew word meaning "to save." The verbal form "to save" is frequently employed in the New Testament, though Jesus is rarely called the Savior.[3] The latter usage would have been familiar to the Graeco-Roman world where gods and emperors also were styled savior, perhaps with a view to the return of the golden age. Thus Caesar Augustus was styled Savior.

To Christians, Jesus is the Savior. Early on, Paul wrote to the Christians at Philippi of the Lord Jesus Christ who is the Savior whom we await from heaven, our true commonwealth (Phil 3:20). The reference to Jesus awaited as Savior is especially appropri-

---

[2]Political as well as religious factors were at work. Not only was the high priest mediator for the people before God but mediator also before their foreign suzerains.

[3]Among the synoptic writers, only by Luke, 2:11, Acts 5:31, 13:23.

ate to Paul who saw the deliverance of the just reserved to the last when judgment is rendered and the wrath spent (1 Thess 1:10). To Paul the redemption is fully achieved both of man and the universe, the body is made spiritual (1 Cor 15:42-57) and earth made heavenly (Rom 8:18-39), only at that hour to which all creation tends, the Second Coming of Christ. The perspective is somewhat similar in the Pastorals though not entirely so. To Titus that the grace of God has appeared inspires hope that at the last there shall appear the "glory of our great God and Savior Jesus Christ" (Titus 2:13). Yet as is God, Jesus Christ is often simply styled Savior (2 Tim 1:10, Titus 1:4, 3:6).

Origin of Jesus

Joseph is commanded to name the child Jesus "for he will save his people from their sins" (Mt 1:21). The child whose origin is set forth as both human and divine, is included in the Davidic line. For Joseph is himself a son or descendant of David and in naming the child he invokes a paternal privilege. According to Matthew and Luke, and consistently with what they had received from the earliest tradition, Jesus was conceived of the Holy Spirit and born of Mary. Now surely the mystery which encompassed Mary awakened mistrust, apprehension and fear. If God had called Mary, as Joseph perhaps could have surmised even before his dream, then with what fear and trembling would he have approached her. He would hardly have approached her at all. Only God could overcome the fear of Joseph who then, with fear like Abraham's, acquiesced in the divine intervention (Mt 1:20).

Confidence in divine intervention at the birth of Jesus enables the evangelist to introduce the first of the Old Testament prophecies which he now sees fulfilled in Christ: that of Emmanuel or "God with us" (Mt 1:23, Isa 7:14). Both names, Jesus and Emmanuel, have practically the same sense. In Jesus, God is in the midst of his people. Implicit in the name, Jesus, is forgiveness of sins. But the forgiveness of sins is a divine prerogative.

Genealogy of Jesus Christ

An extended genealogy precedes announcement of the birth of Jesus and the mission to save his people from their sins (Mt 1:21).

The ancestry of Jesus is traced back to David and thence to Abraham (Mt 1:1-17). What is reflected in the genealogy is the eternal counsel of God. Hence the birth of him whose life, death, and resurrection flashed to the world the light of that hope long cherished in Israel could not have been without reference to Abraham. He first among men, historically, was called to acknowledge in utter faith the hope inspired by the living God.

In Matthew's genealogy David is juxtaposed to Abraham as a pivotal point in the development of Christ's ancestry. Each inaugurated a series of fourteen generations through which was advanced the promise afforded Abraham and then David. The conclusion of the third series would bring the promise to its fulfillment. The arrangement of the fourteen generations in each series was admittedly artificial. But the succession was preserved and the climactic significance of Jesus underscored.

If both Abraham and David were pivotal points in the genealogy of Jesus, David was the more so. He looked back to Abraham as his ancestor (Gen 17:6). He was anointed king in the very city hallowed by the sepulchre of the patriarch. At the same time at the instance of the prophet Nathan (2 Sam 7), David looked ahead. With his posterity would somehow be linked the inauguration of an everlasting kingdom (cf. Pss 89, 132). The Messiah would be the son of David *par excellence.* In offering unanimous testimony on this point the authors of the New Testament probably reflect widespread sentiment at the time of Jesus.

Son of David

Matthew refers to Jesus as the Son of David twice as many times as do Mark and Luke. He portrays him not so much as that figure of moral earnestness and strength who once prevailed against the enemies of Israel but rather emphasizes David's compassionate stance. Like Mark, Matthew recalls the triumphant salute to Jesus as the Son of David when he enters Jerusalem on Palm Sunday. But Matthew alone of the synoptic writers adds that on this occasion just prior to Jesus' passion and death, there came to him the blind and the halt (Mt 21:14). He healed them as he healed also the distraught. For thus had the youthful David once banished an evil spirit from Saul (1 Sam 16:23). Now Jesus answers the appeal to the Son of David. On one such occasion he heals the possessed daughter of a Canaanite woman (Mt 15:22). On another he heals a demoniac who was blind and dumb (Mt 12:22). To the blind and the halt, to the distraught and possessed, Jesus offered healing and hope.

Similarly did Jesus reach out to sinners. Cumulatively the series of ten miracles recounted in Matthew after the Sermon on the Mount was meant to enhance the sense of the transcendent authority of Jesus. At the same time the object of his healings included suppliants from beyond the community of the Torah as well as the ritually unclean and inferior. Observe the first three whom Jesus healed in this series: a leper, a Gentile, and a woman. What was asked of them was faith. These Jesus would gather into a new community: the church. ". . . For I came not to call the righteous, but sinners" (Mt 9:13).

Ancestry: Flesh and Blood

To Matthew commentators attribute a profound Christology which emphasizes Jesus' divinity. Yet it is clear that in becoming man Jesus became the true servant of the Lord and assumed the visage of sinful and suffering humanity. In the extended genealogy which preceded the announcement of Jesus' birth and mission were woven the names of patriarchs and kings and, often, the names of sinners. In their succession to David the kings bore the Messianic hope, and yet the lives of such as Ahaz and Manasseh were lived in despair. Then there were the women introduced into the Matthean genealogy: Tamar, Rahab, Ruth and the wife of Uriah, Bathsheba. They were sinners. Something irregular characterized their union with their partners. Nevertheless, these women were brought into the resolution of God's overarching will and counsel.

In retrospect of David's reign, the founder of the tribe whence the king came is invested with a royal and Messianic promise. Yet it is thanks to Tamar that Judah's posterity extended beyond the first generation. Similarly the line issuing finally in David would stand again in peril until Ruth redeemed it, and with that the promise. Rahab, in receiving her unlikely visitors, is remembered as a heroine of faith (Josh 2, Heb 11:31). David sired Solomon through Bathsheba. All of them would seem unlikely agents of the divine counsel, yet they advanced its purpose. When at last the Virgin conceives of the Holy Spirit, the previous episodes all pale beside the resplendent mercy encompassing Mary at Nazareth. "She will bear a son, and you shall call his name Jesus, for he will save his people from their sins" (Mt 1:21).

Heritage of the Nations

Jesus would free not only his own people, the Jews, but all people from their sins. He is a descendant of Abraham but through him is the promise to Abraham fulfilled, that the patriarch's descendants should be as numerous "as the stars of heaven and the sand which is on the seashore" (Gen 22:17 cf. Gal 3:14). The true descendants of Abraham are they who imitate the faith of the patriarch (Gal 3:7, 23-29, Rom 4). The magi can first among the nations lay claim to the faith and patrimony of Abraham. Their long and arduous journey to Bethlehem remains a paradigm to all who would seek Christ in faith. They anticipate the Roman centurion whose servant Jesus heals at Capernaum who will come to sit at the Messianic banquet with Abraham, Isaac, and Jacob, while at the same time the sons of the kingdom are cast out (Mt 8:11, 12). The last is resonant with apocalyptic overtones but at the same time enters into the development of that theme about the rejection of the Jewish nation which perseveres through the gospel.

The Forerunner

"In those days came John the Baptist . . ."

The voice of the Baptist resounded like the roar of the lion above the tamarisks and willows on the river Jordan's banks, "Repent, for the kingdom of heaven is at hand" (Mt 3:2). The harsh and desert wilderness in which he preached above the Jordan cast in dramatic relief the Baptist's own isolation, his timelessness, and the otherworldly burden of his prophetic message. This world seemed to have little claim on the almost spectral figure who lived on grasshoppers and wild honey (Mt 3:4; cf. Mk 1:6). It was as though he were Elijah come back from the dead (Mt 17:10-13, Mk 9:13, Lk 1:17). Hundreds of years had passed since that prophet had uttered his impassioned indictment of Jezebel and her court, but the fire which he brought down upon his enemies (2 Kgs 1:10-12) smoldered still in this latter-day Elijah. The return of Elijah had been long anticipated. From the fifth century before Christ the prophecy was heard, "Behold, I will send you Elijah the prophet before the great and terrible day of the Lord comes. And he will turn the hearts of the fathers to their children and the hearts of the children to their fathers . . ." (Mal 4:5).

These verses of Malachi are the last in the prophetic books. Prophecy then fell quiescent until the appearance of John the Baptist.[4] Through the intervening years the expectation persisted that Elijah would return before the great day of the Lord. When Jesus comes to announce the Day of the Lord and even to set it in motion; to offer grace and at the same time pronounce judgment upon an age long in thrall to sin and death; to proclaim the kingdom of heaven even while warning of the fires of the last day; he acknowledges the Baptist as his Elijah. John was not Elijah, of course, but rather the Elijah of the Messiah. ". . . If you are willing to accept it, he is Elijah who is to come" (Mt 11:14). To the community which Matthew addressed the comparison of John to Elijah would be correlative to its confession of Jesus as the Messiah.

In inaugurating the kingdom to which tax collectors and harlots were called from the bondage of sin (Mt 21:31, 32) and where death itself would yield at the last its claim upon man (cf. Mt 27:51-53), Jesus altered the course of the ages. The kingdom of heaven was at hand and with its very proclamation Matthew associated the Baptist, the latter-day Elijah (Mt 3:2, cf. 4:17). Like Jesus he would pay the supreme price for his preaching. But as Elijah *redivivus* the Baptist was a prophet and "more than a prophet" (Mt 11:9). If all the prophets and the law prophesied

---

[4]Ps 74:9, e.g., and 1 Macc 4:46, 14:41, reflect longing for a new prophet. Luke especially draws attention to the prophetic call of the Baptist, "the word of God came to John the son of Zechariah in the wilderness" Lk 3:2. Cf. Jer 1:1, 2.

until John (Mt 11:13), then like lightning before the storm of glory which was the coming of the Lord the appearance of the Baptist signalled fulfillment of the ancient prophecies: judgment or grace through Jesus Christ. Though still of the past, John the Baptist belongs really to the era of fulfillment (cf. Mt 11:11).[5]

With persuasion and power John touched his peers. All Judea went out to him. He baptized them in the river while they confessed their sins. Did his preaching commence in the Fall of the year when the Jordan flowed more slowly and the sun above abated its fearful summer heat? If so, his preaching would have coincided with the New Year and Yom Kippur or the Day of Atonement. On Jerusalem's heights the great bronze portals of the temple would swing open. Within, amid clouds of incense, the High Priest enters the Holy of Holies and applies to the inner sanctuary the blood of animals. This, to propitiate the wrath of God and to expiate sin, both his own and that of the people. Though the son of a priest, the Baptist had eschewed the Temple. God-stricken, his anointing as prophet derived not from priestly succession but from the living God, immediately and irrevocably. Others in that remote neighborhood about the Jordan also eschewed the Temple. The visionaries at the Wadi Qumran, called Essenes, had retired to the wilderness to spare themselves the corruption of the temple and its illegitimate succession of high priests. There in the wilderness they would await the turning of the ages. They were seekers after holiness for all that they belonged "to wicked mankind, to the company of ungodly flesh" (1QS 11). In place of assisting at the expiatory sacrifices in the Temple they sought rather to offer the sacrifice inherent in a life hallowed by suffering and the exercise of virtue (1QS 8, 9).

Baptism Unto Repentance

At the clarion call, "Repent, for the kingdom of heaven is at hand," Jerusalem, and all Judea, and all the region about the

---

[5]W. Wink, *John the Baptist in the Gospel Tradition* (Cambridge: University Press, 1968) 35, "He stands not on the other side but on this side of the eschatological divide which separates the old from the new time. With his appearance the kingdom begins to arrive." See W. Trilling, "Die Taufertradition bei Matthäus," *BZ* (1959) 286.

Jordan gathered at the river, there to be baptized (Mt 3:5). Following Mark, Luke in his account specified John's baptism as a baptism of repentance "unto forgiveness of sins" (Lk 3:3; cf. Mk 1:4). For John had espied in Jesus the coming of the kingdom, especially the forgiveness of sins. But the forgiveness of sins would not actually transpire except through the death of Jesus. So Matthew transfers the reference "unto the forgiveness of sins" to the last supper when Jesus sets in motion the universal redemption he would achieve on the Cross.[6]

The throng which gathered by the river, John had summoned to a baptism of repentance (Mt 3:11). He proffered a ritual washing to all who would turn to God from sin. Actually lustral washings preceded initiation into the pagan mysteries, such as the Eleusinian or those of Isis and Mithras. But for the most part, to the crowds who attended John, the pagan mysteries lay on *terra ignota.*

Yet even in Palestine ritual ablutions were well established in Jewish and Gentile practice. So John was not alone in proposing to his followers some form of ritual washing. The significance of these washings would differ. Some could even be compared to the ablutions which the Moslem performs before prayer or to the aspersion of Christians before Mass.

> "You shall sprinkle me with hyssop, O Lord, that I may be purified: Wash me, and I shall be whiter than snow" (Ps 51:7).

Generally conversion and moral orientation could be presupposed among the Jews. The deep sense of God in the Hebrew religion, and a strong sense of guilt which prevailed in the post-exilic period, demanded conversion. This was true among the visionaries at Qumran. Thus, the Community Rule:

> "They shall not enter the water to partake of the pure Meal of the saints, for they shall not be cleansed unless they turn from their wickedness; for all who transgress his word are unclean" (1 QS 5:13, 14).

[6]J. Meier, "John the Baptist in Matthew's Gospel," *JBL* 99 (1980) 388.

It was true of John the Baptist. His coming signalled fulfillment of the ancient prophecies: judgment or grace through Jesus
Christ. The turning of the ages was at hand. Weaving into his
preaching such apocalyptic motifs as wrath and judgment, the
Baptist's voice awakened the consciousness of the people from
the Jordan valley to the heights of Jerusalem. In the light of the
coming judgment baptism would be "a dramatic piece of prophetic symbolism," an antidote to the wrath, somewhat akin to
the blood smeared on the lintel at the original Passover, and to
the mark of which Ezechiel wrote.[7] To be an antidote to the wrath,
however, John's baptism would necessarily be a baptism unto
repentance. Jesus acknowledges it. He submits, thus "to fulfill
all righteousness" (Mt 3:15).[8] At first the Baptist demurred. Jesus
ought to baptize him, not vice versa (Mt 3:14). Yet thus ritually
would Jesus associate himself with the generality of men and
women, men and women who are sinful and beset with weakness.
The theophany which follows relates Jesus to the living God.

Hence whatever Jesus says or does, even to the forgiveness of
sins, is ratified in heaven. The heavens open and the Spirit of God
descends "like a dove" (Mt 3:16). Had not Jesus been conceived
within the very ambience of the Spirit? The creative agency of
God is at work. Now that Spirit anoints Jesus. Concomitantly
a voice from heaven thunders, "This is my beloved Son, with
whom I am well pleased" (Mt 3:17).

Now as the true Son of the Father in heaven Jesus would live
his life obediently, even to his death on the Cross. All who sub-
mitted to the baptism of John would orient their lives anew. They
would follow John on the way to righteousness (Mt 21:32) and
bring forth fruits befitting repentance. They would reflect a degree
of inner goodness as well as obedience. Thus will harlots and tax
collectors enter the kingdom of God before the proprietors of the
Jewish nation and tutors to its soul. For the latter put no cre-

[7]A. D. Nock, *Early Gentile Christianity and its Hellenistic Background* (New York: Harper
& Row, 1964) 124.

[8]B. Przybylski, *Righteousness in Matthew and His World of Thought* (Cambridge: University Press, 1980), ". . . in 3:15 righteousness does not refer to the gift of God but to God's
demands upon man. John and Jesus are to carry out the total will of God." 94.

dence in John (Mt 21:31, 32). Yet all this would not be possible apart from that reservoir of divine mercy and forgiveness which was drawn upon when Jesus mounted the Cross. From this supreme sacrifice of love the baptism of Jesus derives its fire. It evokes from the Spirit the divine largesse . . . "I baptize you with the Holy Spirit and with fire" (Mt 3:11). Fire is often associated with judgment in the Bible. That may be the case here in a context so redolent with an apocalyptic coloring (Mt 3:10, 12). Yet the association of fire with the Holy Spirit in both Matthew and Luke (Lk 3:16) could allude to the descent of the Spirit in the tongues of fire of Pentecost (Acts 2:3). But allusion to the Pentecost tradition would seem anachronistic on the lips of the Baptist. More likely the judgment in question, if it is a judgment, would imply forgiveness from sin even as the grace of the Spirit is infused. Such grace can transform the heart of man. It implies forgiveness and enables a man to forgive his brother "from his heart" (Mt 18:35). It leads to purity of heart and that blessing reserved for those whose inheritance is the kingdom of heaven (Mt 5:8).

"I desire mercy, and not sacrifice."

Twice the evangelist introduces into the tradition deriving from Mark the divine volition voiced by Hosea, the first of the minor prophets, "I desire mercy, and not sacrifice" (Hos 6:6). In the first instance the text elaborates upon Jesus' reply to the question of the Pharisees as to why he eats with tax collectors and sinners. He is a physician to souls, especially to those in need. As such he ministers in the name of mercy as God wills (Mt 9:10-13).

On the second occasion the sentiment is brought forth to explain his abrogation of the law relating to the Sabbath. In placing the imperative of mercy before the traditional interpretation of the Sabbath law, he acts consistently with the perennial disposition of the living God. Jesus cannot do otherwise. He is lord of the Sabbath (Mt 12:8). It is the Pharisees who ironically in their devotion to the law contradict the law and the prophets.

For over a thousand years the Sabbath observance had obtained in Israel. Men rested on that day which was sanctified unto the

Lord. In time Sabbath observance became the distinctive sign of the covenant and rules to prevent an affront to its holiness became stricter and stricter. To pluck grain was considered reaping, one of the thirty-nine tasks explicitly forbidden on the Sabbath.[9] Similarly, it was forbidden to eat anything not prepared on the day previous to the Sabbath.[10] That the disciples of Jesus should have violated this rule invited the protest of the Pharisees.

Had not David in his time appeared to have similarly affronted the Sabbath?[11] Did he not appear to have violated the sanctuary? David and his men were hungry. So he "entered the house of God and ate the bread of the Presence" (Mt 12:4, cf. 1 Sam 21:1-6). Yet the peril of sacrilege was lessened because David and his men had kept themselves from women (1 Sam 21:5), a condition to approach holy things (Ex 19:15). Perhaps to temper the judgment due the disciples' violation of the Sabbath Matthew mentions that the disciples of Jesus were hungry. In those circumstances even the Pharisees ought not to have protested since "whenever there is doubt whether life is in danger this overrides the Sabbath."[12] There remains in any case the overriding example of David whose transgression of a cultic *tabu* was only apparently such. The Davidic example, according to Matthew, was consistent with the word of God set forth through the prophet Hosea, "I desire mercy and not sacrifice" (Mt 12:7, cf. Hosea 6:6). In case of conflict between the law or sacrifice, and deeds of mercy, the latter takes precedence. Such an example Jesus could evoke with consistency, for as the Son of David he would recall the compassion with which the king would sometimes address his peers.

For all the relevance of the example it was not enough to challenge an authoritative or rabbinic interpretation of the law.[13] This could have been done only by appeal to the law itself. So

[9]*Sabb.* 7:2. See J. M. Hicks, "The Sabbath Controversy in Matthew: An exegesis of Matthew 12:1-14," *Restoration Quarterly* 27 (1984) 81; DeVaux, *Ancient Israel* 483.

[10]*Sabb.* 19a; *Jub.* 2:29.

[11]The text does not say that it was on the Sabbath when David "entered the house of God and ate the bread of the Presence" (Mt 12:4) but presumably it was. See Hicks, *The Sabbath Controversy* 84.

[12]*Yoma* 8:6.

[13]Haggadic teaching centered around the use of examples. They "might serve to inculcate

Matthew adds a further point to justify the disciples of Jesus. ". . . Have you not read in the law how on the Sabbath[14] the priests in the temple profane the Sabbath, and are guiltless?" (Mt 12:5). Matthew thus draws on the commandment of Leviticus according to which the priests must violate the Sabbath while fulfilling the temple ritual. If in the past the Sabbath observance could have been subordinated to the temple observance then that would be true in the time of Jesus. For "I tell you something greater then the temple is here" (Mt 12:6). The temple in Matthew's day was in ruins. But Jesus had succeeded to the temple. In him men and women would have access to God. If the Sabbath observance had been somehow subordinated to the temple in the past, now it was subordinate to Jesus. The Son of Man is lord of the Sabbath (Mt 12:8). This sentiment is found in each of the synoptics but it is especially appropriate to the high Christology of Matthew. Probably something even more disturbing than the revolutionary actions of Jesus and his disciples, and more than the dispute over the Sabbath observance, moved the Pharisees to take counsel to destroy Jesus (Mt 12:14). It was what his words and his actions implied. The church understood. And the swift acknowledgment that Jesus was lord of the Sabbath, led the nascent church to set aside the old Sabbath which had stood for over a thousand years and to defer to the new, the first day of the week, the Lord's Day.

Jesus did not come to set aside "the law and the prophets." He came to fulfill them. As their fulfillment, Jesus is often cast in Matthew as the interpreter of the law and the prophets. Hence in Jesus' dispute with the Pharisees he could invoke the prophet Hosea against them. The use of Hosea 6:6, "I desire mercy and not sacrifice," is unique to Matthew however. Indeed the origin of both 9:13 and 12:7 probably lies with the evangelist.[15] He was

moral lessons, general religious truths and wisdom, and they might also serve to illustrate and corroborate a halakah. But it could not be used to justify the abrogation of a law," D. M. Cohn-Sherbok, "An Analysis of Jesus' Arguments Concerning the Plucking of Grain of the Sabbath," *JSNT* 2 (1979) 36.

[14]Lev 24:8; Num 28:9-10.

[15]This, in spite of the opinion of some scholars that the use of Hos 6:6 by Jesus himself is authentic although not on the occasion on which Matthew attributes it to him. E.g., Allen,

addressing a community which, while concerned with the Sabbath observance, was even more concerned with the church's identity vis-a-vis Judaism. The temple lay in ruins and voices in Judaism were beginning to urge the advantage of loving kindness or deeds of mercy over the expiatory ritual of the temple.[16] But within Judaism what could have been said or done in the name of mercy comparable to the words and deeds of the Lord even to those who appeared to affront the holiness of the Sabbath, to "tax collectors and sinners" of all kinds disparate? He will finally expiate sin in his blood.

The usage of Hosea 6:6 in Matthew 12:7 and 9:13 may reflect even a different view of the living God. In latter day Judaism, obedience was the prime preoccupation, not the obedience of faith but the obedience of works exacted by a Torah which encompassed 613 distinct precepts. Such preoccupation was reflected in the fence raised about the law, including the enumeration of 39 tasks forbidden on the Sabbath. It was reflected in the alienation of the righteous from sinners. But Jesus reveals a God of mercy and forgiveness, thus more authentically interpreting the "law and the prophets."[17] He often works his miracles in answer to the suppliant's appeal to the Son of David for mercy (Mt 9:27, 15:22, 20:30, 31). Jesus multiplies the loaves for five thousand as an expression of mercy (Mt 14:14) and similarly, he feeds four thousand (Mt 15:32). The sending forth of his disciples is also grounded in mercy (Mt 9:36).

Jesus recalls Hosea's voicing the divine argument for mercy when reproached for eating with tax collectors and sinners. Matthew was himself a tax collector and the context in which the evan-

---

McNeile, and Schlatter. See David Hill, "On the Use and Meaning of Hosea VI.6 in Matthew's Gospel," *NTS* 24 (1977) 107.

[16]The earliest allusion in rabbinic sources to Hosea 6:6 is attributed to Johanan ben Zakkai who comforts his pupil and fellow rabbi Joshua when the latter bewails the fact that the Holy Place where Israel's iniquities were atoned for has been laid waste, with the words, "My son, be not grieved: we have another atonement as effective as this. And what is it? It is acts of loving kindness, as it is said, 'For I desire mercy and not sacrifice' " (Hos 6:6). See Hill, "Hosea VI.6 in Matthew's Gospel," 108.

[17]G. Barth, "Matthew's Understanding of the Law," *Tradition and Interpretation in Matthew* (tr. Percy Scott; Philadelphia: Westminster Press, 1963) 83; W. Grundmann, *Das Evangelium nach Matthäus* (Berlin: Evangelische Verlagsanstalt, 1972) 322.

gelist recalls the verse from Hosea follows immediately upon the call of Matthew. He is among those who will share Jesus' authority over sin and the demonic (Mt 10:3). Whether in this scene, where he is called to follow Jesus, Matthew is to be identified with Levi, the son of Alpheus (Mk 2:14; Lk 5:27), or whether in the mind of the evangelist he supplants him, he is a publican and tax collector. He is a member of a despised class in Palestine, a leech on the body politic. Because their property often derived from extortion, tax collectors were a constant affront to the mass of people. In the eyes of the Pharisees the tax collectors were inveterate sinners whose way of life fundamentally contradicted the Torah. Even so Jesus calls Matthew to be his follower (Mt 9:9). That Jesus called Matthew to be one of the twelve (Mt 10:3) was perplexing, if not offensive, to the religious authorities of Judaism. The call and response of Matthew is not as succinctly put as the call of the fishermen. Yet it has a typical ring about it (cf. Mt 4:18-22). ". . . And he said to him, 'Follow me.' And he rose and followed him" (Mt 9:9). Like his summoning of the fishermen, Jesus speaks directly and authoritatively. The call can be compared to the call of the prophets. It cannot be compared to the rabbinical school where the learner offers himself to the teacher, though in following Jesus also a conversion is implied.

Like Peter and Andrew, James and John, Matthew now becomes a fisher of men, (Mt 4:19), a catalyst of the divine mercy which will not be constrained. Many of Matthew's peers will come and sit down to eat with Jesus and his disciples (Mt 9:10). That Jesus would eat with tax collectors and sinners provokes the Pharisees (Mt 9:11). The charge will later be made that he is a "friend of tax collectors and sinners" (Mt 11:19). He receives them in the name of mercy. This sentiment pervades the entire section 9:10 through 9:34 which appropriately follows the healing of the paralytic and forgiveness of his sins. Employing a rabbinic formula Jesus advises his adversaries "Go and learn what this means, 'I desire mercy and not sacrifice' " (Mt 9:17; Hos 6:6).

5

Healing and the Forgiveness of Sin

Jesus embodied mercy. In the second of Matthew's summary statements recalling Jesus' words and deeds, the evangelist notes that "Jesus healed every disease and every infirmity" (Mt 9:35). He did so as an expression of his compassion (Mt 9:36). At the same time it is the healing of a paralytic and the forgiveness of his sin which enters into the development of the gospel's great theme of forgiveness and reconciliation.

The healing of the paralytic was the sixth in a series of miracles which Matthew narrates following Jesus' Sermon on the Mount. Jesus not only cured the paralytic, he forgave his sins. At the conclusion of the Sermon the crowds were said to be astonished at his teaching. For Jesus taught them "as one who had authority, and not as their scribes" (Mt 7:28, 29). Now his "authority" would be further disclosed through a series of miracles (Mt 8:1-9:34). These miracles or extraordinary works of Jesus do not so much contravene nature as renew a fallen nature. To the evangelist they were meant to enhance the authority of Jesus and in answer to faith, afford access to the kingdom. With one exception they involved healing or exorcisms. The last in the series involved both (Mt 9:32-34).

In the first three Jesus heals suppliants either from beyond the community of the Torah or at least ritually inferior. He heals a leper, a Gentile, and a woman. The woman he heals at Capernaum (Mt 8:14, 15). Peter's mother-in-law had lain prostrate with fever. Remedy lay beyond the skill of physician and power of nature. Jesus but touches her hand and the fever leaves her. The contrast between minimum effort and maximum and disproportionate effect argues to divine power. In this instance the revelation of that power will persevere into the evening darkness (Mt 8:16). "With a word" Jesus casts out spirits and heals all who were sick. Beside the word of Jesus, powerful and as immediately effective as that of the living God, the incantation of magician and exorcist must have appeared labored indeed. To Matthew, it all appeared to be the fulfillment of Old Testament prophecy. As we have seen, Jesus in casting out spirits and healing the sick fulfilled the prophetic vision of the servant of the Lord, "He took our infirmities and bore our diseases" (Mt 8:17; cf. Isa 53:4). Again, the argument that prophecy is fulfilled underscores the further, eschatological, dimension of Jesus' healings.[1] They signal a new age and a new covenant between God and his people with its inherent forgiveness of sins (Jer 31:31-34) and hope in the face of judgment. The kingdom of heaven is at hand. The age to come has dawned.

Stilling of the Storm

The next in the series of Jesus' miracles which the evangelist recounts is a nature miracle. The very winds and the sea obey Jesus (Mt 8:23-27). Although when it transpired in Jesus' public life is uncertain, to the evangelist the miracle is an historical episode of perennial significance. Jesus stilling of the storm recalls the sea becalmed at the voice of the living God.

> "O lord God of hosts . . . Thou dost rule the raging of the sea; when its waves rise, thou stillest them . . ." (Ps 89:8, 9).

Rebuke of the Demonic

If Jesus can thus quiet the fury of nature when "he mounts the storm and walks upon the wind" can he not also rebuke the

---

[1]Though the recreation and renewal which characterize the healings derive ultimately from Jesus' expiatory and redemptive death as the source of the new age, what the evangelist emphasizes here is that even as Jesus' teaching occasioned astonishment, for he taught them *de novo* "as one who had authority, and not as one of their scribes" (Mt 7:29), so too his works evoke wonder and awe not only by reason of themselves but because they represent the fulfillment of prophecy and as such are eschatological data. Grundmann, *Matthäus,* 256.

preternatural? The sequence is similar in Mark and in Luke. Though in Matthew's account Jesus' rebuke of the demonic is the more succinct, it is no less dramatic. The fearful cry of the demons to be cast into swine is answered by Jesus' one word, "Go!" (Mt 8:28-34). Their cry emanated from the tombs like the eerie wail of the night winds before the storm. Now the storm was breaking; the time was at hand; Jesus anticipates the coming judgment. "Go!" He commands the demons and the power which had drained the demoniacs of their very humanity leaps into the swine. The swine stampede and all perish in the depths. Whatever may or may not have accrued to the original account in the course of its transmission, its argument is clear: Jesus prevailed over demonic power. Before this revelation of the numinous, the country trembled (Mt 8:34).

Forgiveness of Sin

. . . Unnatural deeds do breed unnatural troubles; infected minds to their deaf pillows will discharge their secrets. More needs she the divine than the physician. (Macbeth 5:1).

The healing of the paralytic is set forth succinctly and, to the dramatic assertion that Jesus possesses divine authority to forgive sins, it is set forth subordinately (Mt 9:6). Some have argued that the primitive account in Mark (Mk 2:1-12) reflects the intrusion of a pronouncement story on a healing narrative. But the dispute about the authority or power to forgive sin had to be present when the carefully structured conflict episodes in Mark were put together (Mk 2:1-3:6). This is Matthew's preoccupation: the authority of Jesus to forgive sins. He refers to it again at the conclusion to the story. The divine authority is now exercised on earth (Mt 9:8).[2] If we have in the two sayings of Jesus to the paralytic (Mt 9:2 and 6) "a specific interpretation of what Jesus' healing precisely means," then the eschatological burden of the story

---

[2]G. Theissen, *The Miracle Stories of the Early Christian Tradition* (tr. Francis McDonagh; Edinburgh: T & T Clarke, 1983) 176; H. Held, "Matthew as Interpreter of the Miracle Stories," *Tradition and Interpretation in Matthew*, 176.

is underscored.[3] Forgiveness of sins characterizes the new age and is integral to the Gospel. Although forgiveness of sins was set forth in the Old Testament and even human mediation was known in the intertestamental period,[4] forgiveness was but provisionary in view of the merits of Christ.[5] Matthew specifies that the blood of the covenant is being poured out for the forgiveness of sins (Mt 26:28).

The wages of sin is death (Wis 1:16, Rom 1:32, 6:23). In the Bible no attempt was made to interpret death as a natural process and thus to neutralize it. It is the signal and universal expression of the divine wrath (Rom 5:12, 16, 18; cf. Gen 3:17-19). Similarly disease, as the counterfeit and mask of death, was deemed an expression of retribution due sin. So argued Job's friends (Job 4:7, 8), the disciples of Jesus (Jn 9:2), and implicitly the letter of James (Jas 5:15). Sin begets sin and reaps an awful retribution in increasing bondage to its fatal power. From moral depravity can issue disease of mind and body. Yet the principle of a transcendent moral order that argues for strict justice and for the punishment to fit the crime, cannot be applied to the human situation in an exclusive and surface way. Job did not do so. Neither did Jesus. Jesus came to save us from our sins.

The unspoken faith of the stretcher-bearers was evident (Mt 9:2). The paralytic was apprehensive. His faith and hope in what would surpass all natural expectation was also unspoken. Yet could he who shared in the love of his friends not share also something of their faith and hope? Passing over for the moment the burden of the young man's physical paralysis, Jesus addresses

[3]B. Gerhardsson, *The Mighty Acts of Jesus according to Matthew* (Lund: Gleerup, 1979) 76.

[4]A fragmentary text from Qumran "The Prayer of Nabonidus" alludes to the forgiveness of sin in God's name by a human being. In 11Q Melch, Melchizedek as a heavenly figure is an agent expiatory of the sins of his people. See J. A. Fitzmyer, "The Aramaic Language and the Study of the New Testament," *JBL* 99 (1980) 15-17.

[5]Cf. e.g., the pre-Pauline formula in Rom 3:25, 26. The thematic scheme which dominates Romans is the eschatological revelation of the "righteousness of God" made effective for man by his acceptance of this revelation or his submission to this righteousness in faith (Rom 1:17, 3:21, 22, 26; 10:3). Two thematic matrices which can be found in Rom 5:9, Christ's sacrificial death and man's being made righteous by faith, are caught in a single participial phrase "Made righteous now by his blood" (Rom 5:9). B. F. Meyer, "The Pre-Pauline Formula in Rom 3:25-25a," *NTS* 29 (1983) 198-208.

himself to the greater burden of sin. To the paralytic he says, "Take heart, my son; your sins are forgiven" (Mt 9:2). That sin to which the human condition has been inured from the beginning, is being remitted the paralytic. His affront to holiness pardoned and his guilt expiated. Banished is the spectre of avenging furies and even demonic possession. The long night is over. Morning has broken. In the light of such deliverance, Jesus can dissolve the lesser bonds with which the man was bound to his bed. "Rise up, take up your bed and go home" (Mt 9:6).

To Jesus' contemporaries and to their posterity this healing of the paralytic signalled "that the Son of Man has authority on earth to forgive sins" (Mt 9:6). The very attribution of the title Son of Man to Jesus in this context has provoked much comment. In the pre-Markan tradition it may have meant simply a human being, that as a man Jesus exercised his divine authority to forgive sins. For the title lends itself to this understanding even as in other contexts Son of Man can refer to Jesus' second coming, after "one like a Son of Man" in Daniel 7:13. In still other contexts it refers to the impending passion and death of Jesus, the price of bringing heaven to earth, and to men the authority to mediate divine forgiveness. "When the crowds saw it they were afraid, and they glorified God, who had given such authority to men" (Mt 9:8). The acclamation differs from the earlier account in Mark where it was directed to the physical healing itself (Mk 2:12). Here within the nascent church what evokes wonder and praise is the attribution to men of the divine authority to forgive sins. The forgiveness which Jesus mediated is now being mediated through the church. Consistently with the will of its founder the church perseveres as an agent of reconciliation. In the first instance it was presumably the twelve upon whom devolved the authority to forgive sins.

Earlier in the gospel, in the context of the missionary discourse, Jesus had given the twelve authority to exorcise the demonic and to heal "every disease and every infirmity" (Mt 10:1). Subsequently the authority and the power to forgive sin appears to devolve upon the twelve. In chapter eighteen of Matthew the twelve would represent the church which, in this case, in its particular communities, is permitted the authority "to bind or to loose" or in the immediate context, to excommunicate (Mt 18:17, 18). In rabbinic usage "to bind or to loose" refers to whether or not the Torah binds in particular circumstances.[6] The usage can also refer to imposing or removing a ban, to expelling from or receiving back into the congregation. This latter meaning the evangelist has in mind in chapter eighteen which relates to church order. That the local church possessed this authority appears to be the case from Paul's first letter to the Corinthians. In a case of incest the sinner was excommunicated from the church. Paul himself had rendered judgment by virtue of his apostolic authority: the sinner was to be delivered over to Satan "for the destruction of the flesh, that his spirit may be saved on the day of the Lord Jesus" (1 Cor 5:5). The apostle chides the church in Corinth for not having made such a judgment and then the Corinthians are expected to carry it out. In the Pastorals a certain Hymenaeus and his fellow Alexander are "delivered to Satan." They had spurned the voice of conscience and then apparently suffered the loss of their faith (1 Tim 1:19, 20). The judgment was actually confirmatory more than anything else. Grave sinners through their implicit denial of God have already passed within the realm of evil. Demonic power can make itself felt only on those who have given themselves up to it.

Those who turn to Christ in faith are loosed from their sins. As is clear from John 20:23 "to bind or to loose" refers also to the forgiveness of sins or to the denial of forgiveness.[7] In the fourth gospel the power to forgive sins is entrusted to the apostles through the Holy Spirit. According to Luke the final commission given the twelve is to preach repentance and forgiveness of sins to all nations in the name of the crucified and risen Lord. This they will do when empowered by the Spirit (Lk 24:45-49).

The twelve function as a kind of transparency to the disciples at large. For other disciples of Jesus will share their power. In the first flush of enthusiasm in the wake of the Resurrection, forgiveness of sin is preached abroad by the twelve and their successors. Just as the authority of Jesus to teach and to heal was

[6]Büchsel, "deō," *TDNT* 2 (1964) 60, 61.

[7]Grundmann, *Matthäus* 392.

imparted to the twelve and then to the disciples at large with a view to the Gentile mission where the waiting fields were ripe for harvest, so is the authority to forgive sin transmitted unto the generations. If the twelve represent a kind of transparency to others who see in them the revelation of Jesus' high and graceful purpose, then Peter can be exemplar to all. It is Peter whom the Lord commands to forgive his brother seventy times seven and to whom he commends the parable on the unmerciful servant (Mt 18:21, 22, 23-35). The pericope preceding the parable and the parable itself reiterate that the quality of mercy should lie behind Peter's "binding and loosing," as well as behind that of the twelve and the disciples through the succeeding generations. The latter will represent the church in its mission of forgiveness and reconciliation. Who they will be will remain within the purview of the church. The mission of forgiveness and reconciliation was and is to continue, so much the more so in view of the persevering struggle between unregenerate man and the spirit; the pervasiveness of sin even within the church; and the need of absolution for sins committed after Baptism.

Rebuke of the Demonic

Forgiveness of the sinner denies the devil his prey. As the ancients believed in a general association of sin and disease, so similarly would they ascribe both to demonic influence. As we have seen in Jewish tradition, sin as *anomia* found its origin and pattern in that mysterious malevolence which from before the beginning of time pitted itself against the Creator. Jesus must contest that malevolence. Even as his public ministry begins, the light of Christ penetrates the recesses of hell. The synoptic gospels agree that at this point the devil, who in rabbinical lore was thought to frequent the desert, comes forth to challenge Christ.

Jesus is "led up" to an ecstatic and visionary plane to engage in an apocalyptic, if not cosmic, struggle against evil (Mt 4:1). The temptations are all said to begin and end in the desert in spite of the physical movement from place to place set forth in the narrative. To be sure the temptations set out in this prologue to Jesus' public ministry will persist through the rest of his history and that of the church. Only here, against a stark and desert background, does Matthew cast Jesus and Satan in such a titanic struggle. The tempter offers finally all the kingdoms of the world in barter for Jesus' homage (Mt 4:8, 9). Jesus refuses. The tempter is dismissed. For Jesus is more radically the ruler of all. In time he would ascend the mountain to assert his sovereign authority (Mt 17:1-7, 28:16-20). The psalm once chanted on the occasion of the succession to the throne of David would now ring especially true,

> . . . You are my son, today I have begotten you. Ask of me, and I will make the nations your heritage, and the ends of the earth your possession (Ps 2:7, 8).

Yes, beyond the ends of the earth, beyond the ramparts of this world, beyond universe after glittering universe extends the sovereignty of Jesus Christ. The dismissal of Satan (Mt 4:10) at the beginning of Jesus' mission on earth says something of his sovereignty vis-a-vis the preternatural. It anticipates the sentence to be pronounced irrevocably at the last when Jesus will cast the devil and his legions into hell (Mt 25:41).[8] It anticipates that victory which all who acknowledge him are called to share.

Surely the presentiments of that victory were many and varied in Jesus' passage on earth. ". . . If it is by the Spirit of God that I cast out demons, then the kingdom of God has come upon you" (Mt 12:28). In the first summary of Jesus' activity, besides teaching and preaching the gospel of the kingdom, he is said to heal all the sick brought to him: the diseased, the lame and the halt, and demoniacs (Mt 4:24). Similarly in the cycle of miracles recounted in chapters eight and nine, when the first triad concludes, Matthew again alludes to the power of Jesus over demons mediated "with a word". At the same time the evangelist describes the universal reach of Jesus' healing power (Mt 8:16). Now the connection presupposed between disease and sin can account for the marked frequency of demonic possession in the gospel narrative. Conditions which today could be subject to medical analysis and amelioration were sometimes ascribed to preternatural

---

[7]That angels presently appear to minister to Jesus after the tempter leaves further enhances the sense of Matthew's high Christology.

influence. The general association between disease and sin was so widespread as to make plausible the attribution of both to demonic influence. In Matthew 17:15, for example, the boy is said in the Revised Standard Version to have been an epileptic. According to Matthew the boy was touched, moonstruck, or a lunatic (in Greek "selēniazetai"). The symptoms are similar. Lunar emanations were then esteemed harmful (cf. Ps 121:6). Hence the spiritual force which was thought to inhabit the heavenly spheres, albeit malevolently, must be brought to bear and rebuked. The object of exorcism is greater than flesh and blood. In any case the miracles of Jesus were an attack on the power of Satan, be it real or sometimes merely reputed and yet still real to the minds of men. When the disciples could not prevail on such a plane, it was because they did not have sufficient faith (Mt 17:19, 20).

The series of miracles which Matthew introduced in chapters eight and nine to enhance the authority of Jesus concludes with an exorcism. One whose voice is mute and whose tongue is held in thrall is delivered from his bondage. The demon is cast out and the dumb man speaks (Mt 9:32, 33). The crowds marvel and cry out, "Never was anything like this seen in Israel" (Mt 9:33). No, never seen was the impressive accumulation of works which Matthew sets forth in chapters eight and nine of his gospel. Even the enemies of Jesus conceded that the inspiration of his works was at least preternatural. To the Pharisees, Jesus was a sorcerer (Mt 9:34).

The crowds were not persuaded by the charge of the Pharisees. In a subsequent exorcism resulting in restored sight as well as speech, the crowds ask, "Can this be the Son of David?" (Mt 12:23). Again the enemies of Jesus accuse him of sorcery. "It is only by Beelzebul, the prince of demons, that this man casts out demons" (Mt 12:24). On this occasion Jesus would answer his enemies. Still, the calumny lingers on. The works remain also, to be interpreted in Jesus' time as in generations thereafter. To the crowds who attended Jesus, surely his works suggested that the Messianic age was dawning, that the reign of God was beginning; to his enemies in their prejudice and malice, that Jesus mediated even demonic power; and to his followers, especially in the light of his resurrection, that his interventions were divine.

The faith of the suppliants in the several miracle stories re-counted in chapters eight and nine appears already to have recog-nized that the central mystery of the person of Jesus exceeded the comprehension of the crowds and much more so that of the spiritual authorities of Judaism. Logic would destroy the argu-ments of the latter: "If Satan casts out Satan, he is divided against himself; how then will his kingdom stand?" (Mt 12:26). The king-dom of God will stand. In its light demons are cast out; sins are forgiven men. Granted the influence of the devil which a long Jewish tradition esteemed him to have had on human beings,[9] then for those who adhere to Christ that malevolent influence stands rebuked.

If in Israel a demonic mythology was widespread in the inter-testamental period, it was much the more so in the world at large. Among the Jews speculation about demons pervades the books of Enoch, Jubilees, and the Ascension of Isaiah, for example, as well as the Dead Sea Scrolls. Like angels, demons were almost universally acknowledged in the world at large. The "thrice ten thousand spirits which Zeus had sent on earth as watchers of mor-tal men,"[10] had their counterpart in the legion of demons which beset men. Farther to the East in Iranian religion the army of angels attending Ahura Mazda had its counterpart in the legion of demons marshaled with Ahriman, the evil spirit. At the time of Jesus the occult exercised a deep fascination expecially beyond Israel. Magic and astrology were elevated to sciences or pseudo-sciences. Incidents of possession were frequent enough. But their hour had come: "What have you to do with us, O Son of God? Have you come here to torment us before the time?" (Mt 8:29). The judgment was being set in motion. According to Jewish apocalyptic the relative liberty of the demons would one day cease forever.[11] It is perhaps to that time the demons refer, the hour of the redemption (Col 2:15).[12] As we have seen, the exorcism which Jesus worked for the demoniacs amid the tombs at Gadara,

[9]Gen 3:13; Wis 2:23, 24; 2 Cor 11:3.

[10]Hesiod, *Works and Days* vv. 252-258.

[11]Cf. 1 Enoch 16:1; 1QS 3:24ff., 4:18-20; Mt 25:41; Rev 20:10.

[12]See Held, "Matthew as Interpreter of the Miracle Stories," 269, 270.

a city of the Decapolis in the Transjordan, was apparently the first he wrought beyond the land of Israel. A summary account of his ministry at its beginning suggests that already Jesus' fame had spread "throughout all Syria" (Mt 4:24) and that great crowds followed him "from beyond the Jordan" (Mt 4:25). Those who sought out his healing and deliverance included even Gentiles from as far away as Damascus. The mission of Jesus, however, and that of the twelve with him, the object of their preaching, their teaching and their works, is first the lost sheep of the house of Israel (Mt 10:5, 6). So Jesus rarely ventures beyond the land of Israel but when he does do so, his fame precedes him. Such was the case when he repaired to the district of Tyre and Sidon. In the neighborhood of those great port cities lingered the remnant of an old and decadent race. No match herself for the devil, a Canaanite woman seeks out Jesus. Would he in his compassion exorcise the demon possessing her daughter? Remarkably she addresses him as Lord and Son of David, that is, the Jewish Messiah. As Son of David and in deference to his nation Jesus replies, "It is not fair to take the children's bread and throw it to the dogs" (Mt 15:26). He acknowledges the Old Testament tradition that the Jews are the chosen even as he adopts their reproach of unbelievers, "dogs." His usage, however, is the Greek diminutive (*kunarion*) which suggests the little dogs to be tolerated in the house with the children.[13] In view of her faith, which like that of the centurion surpasses that of the children of Israel, Jesus accedes to her impassioned plea. The devil is rebuked. The woman's daughter is healed. Jesus acceded as the Son of David who here as elsewhere in Matthew is cast more after the compassionate stance of the legendary king than as the warrior whose campaign secured victory for his nation. As the youthful David once banished the evil spirit from Saul (1 Sam 16:23) so Jesus relieves the Canaanite of demonic possession.

Forgiveness of One Another

> We do pray for mercy and that same prayer does teach us all
> to render the deeds of mercy . . . (The Merchant of Venice 4:1).

[13]O. Michel, "kunarion," *TDNT* 3 (1965) 1104.

Deliverance from demonic possession and forgiveness of sin, the reconciliation to God of an estranged race of men and women: this was to be the issue of Jesus' work and so too of his teaching. Divine grace would provide also for peace on earth.

In the light of the new covenant with its divine promise of forgiveness (Jer 31:34) man should himself be ready to forgive. Indeed the exercise of divine forgiveness appears almost conditional upon our forgiveness of one another. In Matthew, unlike Luke, or even Mark, one petition of the Lord's prayer is reiterated at the prayer's conclusion, ". . . Forgive us our debts as we forgive our debtors" (Mt 6:12). "Debtor" actually becomes "trespasser" when the petition is repeated. Whether debtors to God in view of his supreme gifts of life and liberty or tresspassers upon his prerogatives and law, both are sinners and wait upon his forgiveness.

Similarly ought humans to forgive their fellow sinners their debts and their trespasses against one another. In keeping with the new covenant of forgiveness and reconciliation which Jesus inaugurated, a new race of men and women should arise unlike the old; unlike the publicans and tax collectors who love only those who love them (Mt 5:46) and unlike the pagans who salute only their brethren (Mt 5:47). The new people of God will show forbearance even to their enemies. Thus will they imitate the generous love of the Father who is in heaven.

That Matthew so often refers to the Father *who is in heaven*[14] reflects a typically Jewish acknowledgment of the holiness and transcendence appropriate to the living God. Yet the God of Abraham, Isaac, and Jacob abides mindful of his creatures. Even though the deepest solidarity of men derives from their propensity to sin and prospect of death, ". . . He makes his sun rise on the evil and on the good, and sends his rain on the just and on the unjust" (Mt 5:45). He does not distinguish. How much then should man distinguish? Surely not so much as to deny forgiveness to their brethren.

As we have seen, to the question put by Peter, "Lord, how often shall my brother sin against me, and I forgive him? As many as

---

[14]Eleven times, compared to twice by Mark and once by Luke.

seven times?'' Jesus answers, ''I do not say to you seven times, but seventy times seven'' (Mt 18:21, 22). Thus Jesus would relieve men of that burden of resentment and of that desire for retaliation which fell upon him as the seed of Cain. For once the forge brought the sword into human history, the lust for vengeance could sate itself beyond all bounds.[15] If Cain is avenged seven fold, then his posterity is avenged seventy times seven fold (Gen 4:24).

The blood shed by Cain and his descendants was a portent to the long history of the human race. Only Jesus could lessen its tragic significance when alluding to the boast of Lamech that he would be avenged ''seventy-seven fold,'' Jesus called for forgiveness ''seventy times seven.'' The allusion is uniquely that of the Matthean redaction but consistent surely with Matthew's version of the gospel where forgiveness and reconciliation are brought so much to the fore.

> When mercy seasons justice . . . (The Merchant of Venice 4:1).

The parable that then follows the brief exchange between Peter and Jesus on the subject of forgiveness is also unique to Matthew. In the New Testament the parable generally conveys something of the mystery of the person of Jesus and ''the secrets of the kingdom'' (Mt 13:11).

This parable of the unmerciful servant revolves about the surpassing mystery which encompasses the interplay of judgment and mercy. The king is standing in for God. It is not an unlikely scene in the world of the time of Jesus: that a lesser official of the realm should petition the king for relief from his debt. What does exceed comprehension is the great amount of the debt and even more, the compassion or mercy of the king in forgiving the debt. The king's compassion, however, fails utterly to penetrate the hardened heart of the servant. He appears the very antithesis of the magnanimous man who in both Greek and Jewish tradition is high-minded and generous. Instead of reflecting the mercy which he had received the servant accosts a fellow servant who

[15]G. Von Rad, *Old Testament Theology* (2 vols., tr. D. M. G. Stalker; Edinburgh: Oliver & Boyd, 1962) I 155.

owed him a small debt and harshly demands repayment. It is the merciful, however, who shall obtain mercy (Mt 5:7). The unmerciful servant provokes anew the wrath of his lord.

The parable of the unmerciful servant bears some comparison with that of the laborers in the vineyard (Mt 20:1-16). That too is unique to Matthew. In this parable appeal is made to justice over against the manifest generosity of the vineyard's owner, over against his magnanimity and true compassion to those who were hired at the eleventh hour. To those hired at the eleventh hour the owner of the vineyard pays the same amount as he paid those who labored through the heat of the day. For to offer compensation due only one hour's work would be just, but hardly sufficient. Those who labored through the heat of the day grumble at the owner's generosity. They grumble at the owner of the vineyard and especially at their fellow laborers that having achieved and merited so little they could be so enriched. The parable, however, relates to the kingdom of heaven, even though the figure of the contracting and reckoning with laborers appears pedestrian enough. In relating to the kingdom, the reckoning is translated into a sphere beyond human understanding.

So much more in the parable of the unmerciful servant is the stance of the king so prodigious of forgiveness as to be beyond understanding. Because a parable is meant to engage its hearers, its implication for men and women is clear: ". . . Should you not have mercy on your fellow servants as I have had mercy on you?" (Mt 18:33). Justice alone cannot govern human affairs. The parable concludes a chapter which has its own unity. The demand to pardon the offender (Mt 18:21, 22) or to forgive the debtor (Mt 18:23-35) is not completely detached from the Christian's duty to the "little ones." These little ones must be guarded from the scandalous and from all evil; they must be brought back when straying (Mt 18:1-14). But with these admonitions comes the demand that Christians exercise mercy towards their fellow man (Mt 18:21, 22; 23-35). As we have seen, the motif of judgment looms large in Matthew. Of the one hundred and forty eight pericopes which can be counted in Matthew at least sixty refer to judgment. Such parables as that of the laborers in the vineyard or the unmerciful servant suggest that judgment shall be tempered by mercy, at least for those who themselves show mercy. That Matthew should have been so insistent on this latter point is shown by his redaction of the Lord's prayer. His reiteration of the fifth petition (Mt 6:12, 14, 15) suggests that he was probably addressing a divided community. But the evangelist's address was finally to the world. Matthew's vision of the last and universal judgment is how men and women answered the imperative of love. Because that love should have been directed to the least of Jesus' brethren, the criterion becomes how they would have answered the imperative of compassion and mercy.

6

Ransom for Many

In the complex Christology of Matthew the figure of David looms large. The evangelist refers to Jesus as the Son of David twice as many times as Mark and Luke. We have seen such suppliants as the blind and distraught approach Jesus with confidence, even as the Son of David. To Matthew the title "Son of David" of course implies much more than that Jesus is a healer. He is the Messiah.

That Jesus should heal "all who were sick" (Mt 8:16) and that he came "to give his life as a ransom for many" (Mt 20:28) actually recalls also that venerable but obscure figure of the Old Testament, the servant of the Lord. Jesus will go beyond the servant in the exercise of his power. He will forgive sins.

Servant of the Lord

In the first instance commentators identify the servant with certain of the kings or prophets or even with the true Israel, that is, those Jews, who, by trusting in God in the midst of desolation, rallied the nation in the darkest hour of her history, the exile and Babylonian captivity. Yet the true servant of the Lord will rally more than Israel.

"It is too light a thing that you should be my servant to raise up the tribes of Jacob and to restore the preserved of Israel; I will give you as a light to the nations that my salvation may reach to the ends of the earth" (Isa 49:6).

That the servant of the Lord through his faith and morality should indeed become a light to the nations was the exalted vocation of Israel in the years of restoration. That the Messiah should be called servant of God in Zechariah 3:8 and in Psalm 89:39 lent some support to the Messianic reading of the servant songs in deutero-Isaiah. This appears to be the basis for the Isaiah Targum admitting the identification of the servant in some instances with the Messiah. It would become an option for Christian exegetes.[1]

Mission of the Servant

The role of the servant who "takes our infirmities and bears our diseases" (Mt 8:17; cf. Isa 53:4), Matthew sees fulfilled in Jesus Christ. It is Jesus who relieves the suppliant throngs of their grievous burdens. Though the evangelist could have been following a Targum in citing deutero-Isaiah he probably drew from a Hebrew text very close to our Masoretic text. The Septuagint had spiritualized the verse: "He bears our sins even as he grieves for us" (Isa 53:4). But the thought of Jesus taking upon himself our sins by way of expiating them, while appropriate to the Matthean perspective, is reserved for later in the narrative. Because Jesus came to expiate and atone for sin, however, he is able to relieve humanity of those temporal ills thought to be the penalty and consequence of sin. Because he came to inaugurate in his blood the new covenant (Mt 26:28), he can offer to men and women the blessing inherent in this covenant, the forgiveness of sins. In the New Testament new is *kainos* more than *neos*. And *kainos* is not simply the chronologically new as second follows first, but rather epitomizes the issue of that divine intervention which, while signalling the end of time and history, introduces the new and everlasting.[2] "Behold! I am doing a new thing . . ." (Isa 43:19).

---

[1]D. Juel, *Messianic Exegesis: Christological Interpretation of the Old Testament in Early Christianity* (Philadelphia: Fortress Press, 1988) 126. Though challenged by such scholars as Barrett, Hooker and Williams, the opinion maintained by Jeremias, Lindars, North, and Taylor remains the more prevalent, that the figure of the Servant of the Lord, the "Ebed Yahweh," especially the suffering servant of Isaiah 53, influenced Jesus' expression of his own vocation and even more, the early church's interpretation of his death.

[2]Nock, *Early Gentile Christianity* 131.

Yet the new is rooted in the old. Israel was a people of promise. The words of Israel's prophets were uttered either in judgment or promise. Neither in vain. The everlasting compassion of the living God who reached out to Abraham, Isaac, and Jacob, and then encompassed an enslaved people could not be constrained. The nations are summoned to share the fulfillment of Israel's promise (cf. Eph 2:11-22). Surely Matthew is an apologist for the fulfillment of Israel's promise in Christ. The new is rooted in the old. The visage wherewith Christ was preached to the world ought not have been thoroughly unfamiliar to the Jews.

When Matthew alludes to the servant songs to what extent does he recall them in his appraisal of Jesus' life and mission? Surely his citations suggest how at least certain aspects of the servant are fulfilled in Jesus. Thus is the servant's healing role recalled in the universal reach of Jesus' healing (Mt 8:17 of Isa 53:4). Similarly does the meekness and humility of the servant presage that of Jesus. So too does the extended impact of the servant's law (Isa 42:4) suggest the universal reach of Christian hope (Mt 12:21).

What is the occasion in which Matthew sees fulfilled the promise inherent in the servant's meekness and humility? Jesus had just commanded silence of those whom he healed (Mt 12:16). The reason he did so is really not that of Mark's whose order Matthew follows through verse thirty-three of chapter twelve. He did so because the Pharisees were taking counsel against him "how to destroy him" (Mt 12:14). At the same time the command of silence afforded a point of departure for citations from the servant poems suggesting Jesus' own reticence and forbearance. He does not come primarily as a *theios anēr* or "divine man" of the Hellenistic world: prophet, exorcist, and miracle worker. Though Jesus was all three, he was first God's obedient servant. At the same time he was agent of the Spirit, mediator of divine forgiveness, and instrument of judgment (Mt 12:18, 20). The high Christology which is characteristic of Matthew is maintained through the evangelist's adaptation of Isaiah 42:1. For reference to the servant as "my chosen" Matthew substitutes "my beloved." He does this with a view to the similar expression thundered forth amid the theophanies at the baptism of Jesus (Mt 3:17) and his transfiguration (Mt 17:5). Yet,

"He will not wrangle or cry aloud, nor will anyone know his voice in the streets; he will not break a bruised reed or quench a smoldering wick . . ." (Mt 12:19, 20).

Though Son of God, Jesus would approach the nations with the same meekness and forbearance he approached Jerusalem (Mt 21:4, 5). Jesus and his movement should no more reflect the zealots in Palestine[3] than the pretensions of the "divine men" in the Graeco-Roman world.

Ransom for Many

The demeanor which Jesus would wear was that of the suffering servant. He came "to give his life as a ransom for many" (Mt 20:28). Though some commentators demur, this interpretation of the life and work of Jesus does appear to reflect what was predicated of the servant of the Lord ages before.

> Yet it was the will of the Lord to bruise him; he has put him to grief; when he makes himself an offering for sin. . . . He poured out his soul to death, and was numbered with the transgressors; yet he bore the sins of many and made intercession for the transgressors (Isa 53:10, 12).

The language may differ, but there can be no question about similarity of mission. Like the servant's mission that of Jesus is a saving one; like that of the servant the mission of Jesus is achieved through vicarious suffering; and like that of the servant, it is unto death, an offering for sin. That the Son of Man came to give his life as a ransom for many (Mk 10:45; Mt 20:28) states the soteriological mission of Jesus with a solemnity which will be surpassed only at the last supper. Jesus had earlier made allusion to his suffering and death in the metaphorical language of draining the cup and undergoing a baptism (Mk 10:38). When at the last supper the metaphor is about to be translated into real-

---

[3]F. Hauck and S. Schulz, "praus," *TDNT* 6 (1968) 649; G. Barth, "Matthew's Understanding of the Law," 125-137.

ity, Jesus proffers his blood as the blood of the covenant "which is being poured out for many" (Mk 14:24).[4]

The saying about Jesus giving his life as a ransom for many does not appear in Luke, perhaps because the context in which it is introduced in Mark and in Matthew is in Luke transferred to the last supper. In Mark and in Matthew the statement that the Son of Man came "to give his life as a ransom for many" really epitomizes Jesus' teaching that service is the measure of greatness. Jesus serves even to offering his life's blood. The discussion had arisen when James and John and, in Matthew's account, their mother, had petitioned Jesus for assurance that the apostles would one day reign with him (Mk 10:35; Mt 20:20). The price of such glory is to drink of the cup of suffering and to share the baptism with which Jesus was to be baptized, that is, a baptism of pain. The future belongs to God (Mk 10:40; Mt 20:23). What is needed now is service. Such was the path followed by the servant of the Lord, even unto death. Such was Jesus' path. He came not to be served, but to serve. As his death approached, Jesus delineated that service the more precisely and stated it with a solemnity that would be surpassed only at the last supper. He had come to give his life as a ransom for many. In Luke the whole context about service and its measure of greatness is transferred to the last supper. According to the longer narrative of the last supper favored by most manuscripts (including verses 22:19b-20), the blood of Jesus had already been proffered as a sacrificial offering. It is enough for Jesus then to say, "I am among you as one who serves" (Lk 22:27).

In Matthew the verse looks ahead to that night pregnant with the world's redemption from the power of sin and death, to that night when commenced the immolation of the Son of God. To

---

[4]The Marcan formula over the bread and wine may reflect a Jerusalem liturgy (as Luke and Paul, that of Antioch). But this would in turn echo substantially, at least, Jesus' words at the Last Supper. In Jerusalem, and among Jewish Christians, the historical memory of Jesus would be stressed. Similarly could Mark 10:45 with its reference to the Son of Man and uncertain context in Jesus' public ministry, represent a late redaction which was, however, substantially authentic. A saying such as this, "one of the most important in the Gospels" would be respected in tradition. See V. Taylor, *The Gospel according to Mark* (London: Macmillan, 1953) 444. Did Jesus first utter the logion as "I shall give my life as a ransom for many"? Cf. A. J. B. Higgins, *Jesus and the Son of Man* (Philadelphia: Fortress Press, 1964) 49.

the purpose of the Father in heaven, who would answer as precisely as the Son? To that purpose answered the birth of Jesus as a descendant of Abraham and heir of David, the Messiah. How much more to that overarching and sovereign purpose would answer the death of Jesus! He came to give his life as a ransom for many. Whether or not the ransom paid by Jesus could be considered actually the equivalent to the offering or *asham* of the servant of the Lord, did not the clairvoyance of the Old Testament prophet envision in that mysterious figure the foreshadowing of Jesus Christ? The notion of ransom was not unknown to the world beyond Israel. The very language here employed was employed in reference to the manumission of slaves. Israel itself provided the provenance of the usage. There one may look especially at the songs of the servant of the Lord, which in their lonely and moving splendor prefigure the broadest lineaments of the life of Jesus and his mission. The servant's vicarious suffering and atonement, and then his vindication, transcend the historical events and heroes of ancient Israel. They are concerned with a saving work which could transpire only in the future. This work can be illustrated from the past and especially from the Exodus, but it is something wholly new and ultimate, the work of the redemption.

In the Septuagint the verbal derivative of ransom or in the Greek, *lutron,* is used especially of freeing from bondage or from imprisonment under an alien power.[5] The payment of ransom was really not at issue. For God owned both Israel and the nations. But it cannot be the same with the freeing of sinners. They are alienated from God. They have fallen short of the mark and therefore of the glory of God (Rom 3:23). They stand in his enormous debt, a debt which they cannot of themselves redeem. They are workers of evil. They stand in need of being ransomed from their thralldom to sin and even more from their indebtedness to God.

Blood of the Covenant

Though ransom may not have been at issue on the night of the Jewish liberation from Egypt, that the angel of the Lord passed

---

[5]Dt 7:8, 9:26, 13:5, 15:15, 21:8, 24:18.

over the Jews while visiting judgment upon their taskmasters suggests that the Jews had indeed become the people of God (Ex 19:3-6). Similarly on that holy night recalling Israel's consecration, Jesus would offer his own blood that all men and women might be reconciled to God. ". . . This is my blood of the covenant which is poured out for many for the forgiveness of sins" (Mt 26:28). To Matthew, the death of Jesus is clearly an expiatory sacrifice. It is he who adds to the words over the cup the phrase, "unto the forgiveness of sins" (Mt 26:28). Mark had associated the phrase with John's preaching of a baptism of repentance. Yet John was simply the forerunner. At the last supper Jesus, among men fond to hope and yet fearful of despair, commences the sacrifice to be consummated on the Cross. That the death of Jesus was unto the expiation of sin was early set forth in the church and from the apparently pre-Pauline fragment in Romans 3:25 to Hebrews extends a sound trajectory. At the same time Jesus' sacrifice was an utter oblation, a voluntary holocaust wherein the crucified was both priest and victim, so profound was his acquiescence in the resolution of God's love for man.

The last great discourse of Jesus in Matthew had just concluded with a vision of the last judgment: the parable of the sheep and the goats. Again, what is the criterion by which judgment is to be rendered? It is to be rendered on the basis of how one has answered the imperative of love, even to the least of Jesus' brethren.

Jesus now foresees his own destruction. He says to his disciples "You know that after two days the Passover is coming, and the Son of Man will be delivered up to be crucified" (Mt 26:2). He thus acknowledges the fatal issue of the conspiracy being formed against him by "the chief priests and the elders of the people." At the same time, he interprets the lavish gesture of a woman at Bethany as an anointing for burial. His hour is at hand and one of the twelve shall prove the tragic catalyst. "Friend," Jesus addresses him as he had when he first called Judas to his company, but Judas is neither companion nor friend and the lie he affirmed when he greeted Jesus at Gethsemane denied all meaning to the disciple's life. "Better for that man if he had not been born" (Mt 26:24). Jesus' own death reveals the truth: that God is pleased to receive the blood of his true servant and Son to requite the

blood shed since the fall of man, to forgive us our sins, and
through our redemption from sin, guilt, and estrangement, to reveal anew the love he revealed at creation.

The death of Jesus answered the overarching will of God. Some
time had elapsed since Jesus had uttered the first prediction of
his coming passion, death and resurrection. To Matthew that
marked the beginning of the second major division of his gospel.[6]
In reply to the remonstrance of Peter, Jesus chided the apostle,
". . . you are not on the side of God, but of men" (Mt 16:23).
In going to Jerusalem and the Cross, Jesus was on the side of
God. To Jesus there was a divine necessity to his fatal movement
(*dei*). The necessity to which the evangelist alludes was not that
blind destiny which among the Greeks could reduce men to being
merely passive instruments of an unrelenting and cosmic movement. Rather, it was the eternal will of the Father in heaven who
was summoning the world to salvation or judgment through the
cross of Jesus Christ.

The divine necessity which Jesus answered is reflected in the
bare sentence that "the Son of Man goes as it is written of him"
(Mt 26:24). Though the immediate point of the sentence is to enhance what follows in verse 24, that is, the fate of the traitor,
that the passion and death of Jesus should have been intimated
in the pages of the Old Testament was something congenial to
the early church. To the church any prophecy, any event, any
phrase, was potentially fraught with contemporary meaning. To
the early church typology meant not an exercise of exegetical in-
genuity but the statement of essential supernatural verities and
the disclosure of hidden contents.[7] The promises and prophecies
had to be fulfilled; rather they had been fulfilled and were being
fulfilled "in these last days." To Matthew and his community
especially was it necessary to find the new in the old. As we have
seen his gospel includes at least forty-two explicit quotations from
the Old Testament as compared with nineteen each in Mark and
Luke and only fourteen in John. The Old Testament scripture

---

[6]J. D. Kingsbury, *Matthew: Structure, Christology, Kingdom,* (Philadelphia: Fortress
Press, 1975) 7-25.

[7]Heb 1:2, cf. 1 Cor 10:11; Nock, *Early Gentile Christianity* 127.

was the oracle of God. As to the nativity and naming of Jesus, "All this took place to fulfill what the Lord had spoken to the prophet:

> "Behold, a virgin shall conceive and bear a son and his name shall be called Emmanuel" (Mt 1:21-23; Isa 7:14).

The ancestry of Jesus which Matthew traced at the beginning of his gospel was primarily theological and kerygmatic in its implication. As we have seen what was reflected there was God's eternal counsel. Hence, the birth of him whose life, death, and resurrection afforded the world that hope already long cherished in Israel, hearkened back to Abraham. For it is in Christ that the promise made to Abraham and received in utter faith is finally fulfilled. Nor could the genealogy of Jesus Christ be written without reference to David. With his posterity would somehow be linked the inauguration of an everlasting kingdom (Pss 89, 132). The Messiah would be the expected Son of David.

If the ancestry of Jesus Christ extended itself under divine providence and the birth of the Messiah fulfilled ancient prophecies, then the death of the Messiah would have been foreshadowed in the scripture of his nation. "Hence the Son of Man goes as it is written of him" (Mt 26:24). Yet he goes in utter freedom. Jesus could not be conceived as the prisoner of past utterances, even prophecies. Rather were they written in his light. Of all who have traversed the earth only Jesus could freely accept death as obedience; for ordinary men it is a necessity to which they are appointed by their humanity (Heb 9:27).

> Lo! o'er ancient forms departing
> newer rites of grace prevail . . .

At the last supper Jesus consecrates his body and blood with a view to the sacrifice of the Cross. For the last time he would keep the Passover in Jerusalem.[8] From the remotest time the

---

[8]Whether or not Jesus' last supper was actually the Passover meal is questioned by some commentators today. That it was so, is most recently defended by Rudolph Pesch and I. H. Marshall. Even if the last supper was originally another type of festive or solemn meal, it would have contained Passover motifs because of its proximity to the observance itself.

firstling of the flock was offered by shepherds to ward off evil; then by the Jews, that the angel of the Lord executing divine vengeance upon the Egyptians would pass over the Jews themselves. Now the true lamb of God was being sacrificed for the people. For those who would scorn his blood the sacrifice was fraught with peril. Their awful cry on Good Friday, "His blood be upon us and upon our children" (Mt 27:25), would redound upon their heads. Within a generation the temple was destroyed and Jerusalem reduced.

To that solemn hour when Jesus consecrates his body and blood the evangelist summons voices which though of the past still possessed a telling resonance: Moses and Jeremiah. Long years before, and deep within the Sinai desert, Moses had sealed with blood the covenant between God and his people (Ex 24:8). The blood was that of victims offered to the Lord and thus consecrated. Blood bespoke life. Life in turn derived from God and, hence, victims such as bulls, rams, and turtledoves, would be sacrificed to acknowledge the Lord's dominion over all life. Blood was thought to effect community between God and man. It animated life and, when splashed on the altar which represented the Lord and then sprinkled on the people, the blood somehow associated the two parties in the same life. It sealed the covenant.

New Jesus seals a new covenant in his blood. His followers receive his blood and are thus associated with his life. As Jeremiah foretold, inherent in the new covenant is the forgiveness of sins. For there could be no covenant without healing that alienation from God wrought through sin.

A millennium and more before Jesus' passage on earth God had raised up from their bondage the Hebrew slaves in the Nile delta. He humbled Pharaoh and reduced the colossi of Egypt. He bore his own people on eagles' wings (Ex 19:4, Deut 32:11-12). The deliverance wrought in terms of the old covenant paled beside that of the new. The language of redemption is similar, but the bondage whence God would deliver his people in terms of the

See J. Kodell, *The Eucharist in the New Testament* (Wilmington: Michael Glazier, 1988) 22–36, 42. All accounts of the last supper would have been affected by liturgical practice and reflect the church's deepening understanding of the meaning of the supper.

new covenant was even more profound and unrelenting than that once exacted by the lash of the Egyptians or later by alien powers in the Holy Land itself (cf. Zech 9:11). Through the blood of Christ, God delivers his people from bondage to sin and its mortal retribution; he delivers them from what baleful influence demonic power was esteemed to exert upon the souls of men and women (Col 2:14); he affords them hope in the face of judgment (Rom 5:9). Rabbinic writers had spoken of men healed of their sins in terms of a new creation.[9] The reconciliation of an estranged race whose progenitors had once stood in the shadows of a fallen Eden for fear of God (Gen 3:8), such a reconciliation can indeed reflect the light of a new creation. The thought which Paul stated so succinctly is that of the New Testament generally, ". . . If anyone is *in Christ*, he is a new creation; the old has passed away, the new has come" (2 Cor 5:17).

According to Matthew, intimations of the new creation follow immediately upon the death of Jesus. Like Mark, Matthew recalls the rending of the temple veil but in the latter's account the cosmic and perennial meaning of the crucifixion is set forth in even more dramatic and apocalyptic terms ". . . the earth shook, and the rocks were split; the tombs also were opened, and many of the bodies of the saints who had fallen asleep were raised, and coming out of the tombs after his resurrection they went into the holy city and appeared to many" (Mt 27:51b-53). Men and nature trembled as they entered into a new age of hope; in the wake of Jesus' resurrection from the dead the just were raised and appeared to many; thus to signal in the mind of the evangelist and the church the coming resurrection of all the just. That sentence of death which man had once provoked *in perpetuum,* God now annuls. He forgives us our sins. In his mercy and in that love which is stronger than death (Rom 8:38, 39), he affords a fallen race hope of renewed life and transfiguration.

As Jesus died, the centurion and his company trembled at the foot of the Cross. The earth quaked and death appeared to yield their tenants from the riven sepulchres and tombs. With reverent awe the centurion and his company confess Jesus as Son of God.

⁹Str-B II 421, 422.

They who had mocked Jesus' title as Messiah and king and then nailed him to the Cross, upon his death confessed him of greater origin than even that of the house and family of David. He was Son of God (cf. Mt 22:41-46). Amidst the paroxysm of nature all about them, the centurion and his company stood before the Cross, as before the axis upon which the ages turned. They echoed the earlier confession of Jesus' disciples (Mt 14:33, 16:16), and so testified to the beginning of their faith and hope. Their sins were forgiven them and their long estrangement from our Father in heaven ended.

The centurion was first among the Gentiles to acknowledge Jesus as Son of God (Mt 27:54). To this day, legions have followed him. The insignia he bore was that of imperial Rome and to its capital city Peter and Paul would soon repair. There they would preach forgiveness of sin and reconciliation to God through the Cross of Christ. Peter especially would recall the admonition of Jesus that if his brother should sin against him, he should forgive him not seven times, but seventy times seven (Mt 18:21, 22). For, as we have seen, thus would Jesus answer that lust for vengeance and retaliation so characteristic of the old mankind (Gen 4:23, 24). Has the church sought thereafter to keep faith with Jesus' teaching on forgiveness? Perhaps the great basilica raised over the site of Peter's martyrdom affords an answer.

> "In this vast and hospitable cathedral, worthy to be the religious heart of the whole world, there was room for all nations; there was access to the Divine Grace for every Christian soul; there was an ear for what the overburdened heart might have to murmur, speak in what native tongue it would" (Nathaniel Hawthorne, *The Marble Faun*).[10]

---

[10]Nathaniel Hawthorne, *The Marble Faun* (New York: The New American Library, 1961) 256 (A Signet Classic).

Suggested Readings

Matthew

Jack Dean Kingsbury, *Matthew,* Proclamation Commentary, Philadelphia: Fortress Press, 1977.

John P. Meier, *The Vision of Matthew,* New York: Paulist Press, 1979.

_____. *Matthew,* New Testament Message 3, Wilmington: Michael Glazier, 1980.

Donald Senior, *Invitation to Matthew,* Garden City, New York: Doubleday, 1977.

Miracles

Birger Gerhardsson, *The Mighty Acts of Jesus according to Matthew,* tr. Robert Dewsnap, Lund: CWK Gleerup, 1979.

H. J. Held, "Matthew as Interpreter of the Miracle Stories," in Bornkamm-Barth-Held, *Tradition and Interpretation in Matthew,* tr. Percy Scott, Philadelphia: Westminster Press, 1963, pp. 165–300.

Howard Clark Kee, *Miracle in the Early Christian World: A Study in Sociohistorical Method,* New Haven: Yale University Press, 1983.

Gerd Theissen, *The Miracle Stories of the Early Christian Tradition,* tr. Francis McDonagh, Philadelphia: Fortress Press, 1983.

Parables

Madeleine I. Boucher, *The Parables,* rev. ed., New Testament Message 7, Wilmington: Michael Glazier, 1983.

Charles E. Carlston, *The Parables of the Triple Tradition,* Philadelphia: Fortress Press, 1975.

C. H. Dodd, *The Parables of the Kingdom,* rev. ed., New York: Scribner's, 1965.

Joachim Jeremias, *The Parables of Jesus,* 2nd rev. ed., New York: Scribner's, 1972.

Pheme Perkins, *Hearing the Parables of Jesus,* New York: Paulist Press, 1981.

D. O. Via, *The Parables. Their Literary and Existential Dimension,* Philadelphia: Fortress Press, 1967.

Forgiveness

H. U. Von Balthasar, "Jesus and Forgiveness," tr. Josephine Koeppel, O. C. D., *Communio. International Catholic Review* 11 (1984), pp. 322–334.

William Klassen, *The Forgiving Community,* Philadelphia: Westminster Press, 1966.

Le Pardon. Actes du colloque organisé par le Centre d'histoire des idées (Université de Picardie), Paris: Beauchesne, 1987. For the reader of French, the proceedings of the recent colloquy at the University of Picardy afford a consistent statement on forgiveness. While not a theological exposition as such, the volume does reflect a theological perspective. True and unconstrained forgiveness of sinful man derives finally from the divine grace and compassion revealed in the Bible. And without such grace and forgiveness, reconciliation among men and women appears impossible.